YOU'RE NOT HIGH ENOUGH

7 Keys to Vertical Living

WAVIE ISO LEE

Splash Society Ink Publishing
Dayton, OH

Splash Society Ink Publishing

Copyright © 2023 Wavie Iso Lee
All rights reserved. No part of this publication may be reproduced, distributed or transmitted in any form or by any means, including photocopying, recording, or other electronic or mechanical methods, without the prior written permission of the publisher, except in the case of brief quotations embodied in critical reviews and certain other noncommercial uses permitted by copyright law.

ISBN: 979-8-9879601-0-3 Print
ISBN: 979-8-9879601-1-0 Ebook

Library of Congress Control Number: 2023916832

Published in the USA.

Although I'll no longer see your face,
your memories will continue to live on in me.

I am blessed to have experienced your existence, grandad.

Table of Contents

PREFACE: What is Vertical Living? 1

KEY I: VISIONARY or Dreamer? 13

KEY II: Execute. Complete. Repeat. 51

KEY III: Place. Position. Perform. 75

KEY IV: Master the Step-Back Effect 83

KEY V: Be Driven, Not Motivated 91

KEY VI: Exceed Expectations of the Opposition 99

KEY VII: No Thought is Insignificant 105

Final Thoughts 113

Words I Live By 117

Dedication Page 119

Author Bio 121

PREFACE:
What is Vertical Living?

Simply put, my core definition of vertical living is the continuous evolution of becoming better. Therefore, vertical living has no limits as it is forever increasing.

Vertical living is also considered a lifestyle one should desire and long to possess. This lifestyle is continually experiencing life at the highest level of success and contentment. The results of vertical living can be fully experienced mentally and tangibly (physically).

The very core of a vertical lifestyle stems from a strong belief and conviction that *you make life happen for you rather than let life happen to you*. Therefore, vertical living can't exist without a good attitude and a vertical mindset. Your belief system and conviction of your skills and abilities live in the attitude portion. The mindset portion is behavioral, where your practices and self-discipline are displayed.

Vertical living is a lifelong pursuit.

Every inspirational figure and motivational speaker has championed everyone to chase their dreams. But what happens when you never catch up to that dream? What happens if you get lost chasing the dream? All too often, we've aimlessly chased dreams because there's no real direction, no objective, and—more importantly—no vision.

> *Dreamers chase, while visionaries pursue.*

Vertical living is a living, calculated pursuit of opportunities. Dreams never come true; only opportunities do. I can dream of being a famous Hollywood actor. Still, without positioning myself in front of those opportunities or making myself available for those opportunities, the dream is only a dream.

Vertical living is a perspective.

To truly reach that level of vertical living, you must first experience the downside of experiencing life horizontally. Some of us have journeyed through life, riding the wave of living it forward and backward with a few lateral moves that give off the feeling and idea of advancement. This perspective leads us to believe that we are progressing toward success. However, we are just traveling back and forth, never improving by reaching new heights and destinations.

It could be advantageous for life's challenges to disrupt our horizontal comfort so that we can rise to untapped new heights and discover unique destinations.

In life, many barriers work against the pursuit of vertical living. For example, when you think about a rocket that attempts to blast into space or a jet breaking the sound barrier, many challenges await to resist these vertical efforts. (I'll explain more about this concept in a minute.)

The perspective of vertical living means that you must strive *daily and commit to overwhelming yourself with optimism* from the moment you wake up. Life is perspective; it is the fabric of how you view life. Having an optimistic perspective is how you view a situation, your outlook, and the realization that problems only exist because there is a solution.

PREFACE: What is Vertical Living?

The perspective on the other side of vertical living is that your tribulation is only a momentary situation.

How does one practice vertical living?

I believe it's best to be fully convinced in your abilities to be exactly what you want. This intense practice comes into play mentally—being content and accepting that there's a strong possibility you won't become what you want to be or make it to where you want to go. This idea is very conceivable and worth the discipline so long as you can still operate within the scope of what you desire to become.

You must have the mindset, "Even if that's the case, I'm still going to put in the work, and I'll be open to participating wholeheartedly wherever that effort gets me." Why? This unique perspective still affords you access to vertical living because you're still in the arena of endless opportunities and life-gaining possibilities.

The practice of vertical living grants you the advantage of **responding** to life's challenges and not **reacting**. When reacting, which is purely driven by emotion, you're unaware of alternate positive outcomes or possibilities. This emotional processing of the situation or circumstances fighting against you does not work in your favor and can lead to unwise and instinct-motivated decision-making.

Reacting doesn't gain you any advantages. On the other side of that spectrum is to practice responding; this is a clear indicator that you are still ultimately in control by using your logic, all while your emotions are kept in check. Processing and compartmentalizing raw emotion will allow you to make logically sound decisions. This method will ultimately lead to more beneficial and vertical results.

Vertical living requires breaking the sound barrier in your life—pushing past the obstacles of those challenging barriers you'll come face to face with during your pursuit of living the life of a visionary.

So, allow me to lead off by asking a question.

Are you familiar with how the sound barrier is broken?

If not, that's okay. I'll fill you in on the process.

The sound barrier was once known to the science community as an unachievable, unbreakable, and unmovable force. The idea of an airplane soaring above land was considered a daunting task when the Wright Brothers first envisioned flight. To travel faster than the speed of sound was inconceivable, pushing the envelope of technology.

Before taking flight and breaking any sound barriers in your own life, let's better understand this phenomenon, which Webster's dictionary defines this way: "The sonic barrier ... is a hypothetical barrier to flight beyond the speed of sound; it is so postulated because an aircraft undergoes an abrupt increasing drag force induced by compression of the surrounding air when traveling near the speed of sound."

After knowing that, what are your initial thoughts? Is your mind spinning like mine when I first read this definition? I can only imagine how puzzled and confused you must be about what this has to do with *becoming a visionary, living vertically,* and even more ... *how does this apply to your life?*

If you pondered this and asked yourself that question, I'm glad and hope you're more curious about why I'm also introducing the book with this concept. Stay with me. I'm going somewhere with this thought.

A jet must travel faster than 767 mph to break the sound barrier. Once that jet goes above 767 mph, it creates a force so powerful that it causes a sonic boom, a shock wave resulting in an explosive sound. A dynamic shift occurs once the jet has reached Mach 1—the speed of sound—and broken through the sound barrier. Jets often follow the speed of sound, but once a speed of 768 mph is reached, the sound of speed now follows the jet.

PREFACE: What is Vertical Living?

For us to do groundbreaking work, reach life-changing speeds, and make life happen for you (as opposed to life happening to you), you must become like the supersonic jet: breaking barriers and doing the impossible. The unimaginable. The inconceivable.

A few basic principles must become active to produce noteworthy results. First, you must be renewed and transformed in the mind, heart, body, and soul—enabling you to reach Mach 1 in the flight of life … you lead so that life follows.

When a commercial airline is traveling, our ears first recognize the sound of the airplane. Then, our eyes locate where the sound is coming from. But when a jet breaks the sound barrier, you witness the jet first and then hear the booming sound. This is an example of the intensity and focus you must hunger for and desire to experience Vision and Vertical Living!

You must become that booming sound, breaking all the natural laws life will use to keep you traveling lower than your greatest potential. So, if you feel like you haven't taken flight, keep reading. My prayer and sincere hope would be that you'll soar high by the time you finish this book.

Growing up in Dayton, Ohio, I was always eager to engage in basketball, science, tech, entertainment, and occasionally some mischief. I was an honor roll student, class clown, and 4-star athlete. My upbringing was in a decently warm two-parent home with my little sister. Growing up, I've always possessed leadership qualities, seeking to do things differently than my peers. Put another way, I was always searching for opportunities to innovate their skills while utilizing those same skills to work to my advantage.

As my life evolved, I would find myself associated with many accomplishments and illegal activities, ranging from being honored with the Principal's Award to cooking cocaine into crack and selling just about every narcotic I could get my hands on. As random and exciting as this may sound about my fascinating life journey, unfortunately, you'll have to wait for the autobiography!

Now, I've given you the 411 of my whole jet analogy, and I can sense you're still waiting on that "drop the mic" moment, right? So, here it is made simple! If you are unsatisfied with where you are in your life, then it's clear you're like that jet traveling 767 mph. Recall from my earlier point that it takes 768 mph to break the sound barrier as of this reading.

While keeping that in mind, you are just one mile per hour away from breaking all types of barriers in your life—obstacles holding you back from creating that sonic boom for your vision, aspirations, and, more importantly, your life.

Your sonic boom moment might be a profitable startup business, becoming an impactful mentor, inventing the next big tech boom, or helping lead a positive charge toward social injustice. On the other hand, you may desire a more fulfilled marriage, land a spot on the Forbes 500 list, or add more value to your neighborhood by being a better version of yourself. Could you be fed up with how things are conducted on the Hill in D.C. and ready to emit real change for your community, school system, and diverse cultures? I don't know what you want to do, but I know you're more than capable of achieving what you set, not just your mind but equally *what you set your commitment to.*

Let me ask you a few critical questions.

When did you last have a real heart-to-heart conversation about why you are not living out your passion? How much time do you spend living it in joy each day? What is your definition of *Happiness*?

When I understood that absolute joy is not experienced by a substantial bank account, ultimate success, and an overwhelming amount of material possessions, I knew there had to be a different meaning and something more than just favorable outcomes that create happiness.

PREFACE: What is Vertical Living?

I realized that joy was more important than happiness to me. Joy was to become permanent due to happiness always fleeting and being short-lived. I no longer desire things or outcomes to make me happy because happy results won't always come our way favorably. It is moments and contentment that bring about sustainable and renewable joy. One perspective that frequently comes to my mind is that just because you're alive doesn't mean you're living. Just because you have things or favorable situations that make you happy doesn't mean you have joy.

Your goals are achievable, but your problem is like that jet traveling 767 mph. You have obstacles, distractions, disappointments, crippling habits, and—if I'm honest—too much comfort. In many cases, the trials, shortcomings, and provocations you're facing are often self-inflicted due to a few lacking areas of self-management. Where does this lack most often show up? Maybe it's your deficiency of knowledge, shortage of self-discipline, and self-control. These lapses in verticality are all due to procrastination, ignoring your ignorance, and a failure to face your fears.

But thankfully, there is Someone greater in you than he who is in the world (1 John 4:4). There's a jet inside the encoding of your DNA waiting to be unleashed ... waiting to break barriers.

Have you grown tired of being the poor result of life-hindering thoughts such as "This is just the hand life has dealt me" or "My life is just what it is"? Are you trapped at a "good job," being a "good worker," yet adding no value to your life from the job? Perhaps you've maxed out on your potential by dedicating all your effort, time, and energy to work 60 hours a week. I was never sold on the 30-10-6 combination. The thought of giving a single company 30 years, 10 hours, and six days of my energy, time, and life was a sickening realization. Don't get me wrong, there is a season for this, but it must be met with a different agenda, mindset, and overall objective. Remember, life is not what you make it but what you make happen.

Living life as an empty shell of yourself is not beneficial and is no longer satisfying, especially while seeking a way out. We both know why you could stop moving forward and give up on life, but that's a dead man's mentality with a casket happily awaiting you. When I refer to a casket, I do not mean physical death; I'm implying that living under that old regime of "job, eat, sleep" will put your vision, purpose, and greatness in a casket.

The rationale here is for you to conceptually realize the power you possess to make life happen for you and not allow life to happen to you!

I wrote this book because I was an exact version of what I had to remedy—stop allowing life to happen *to* me instead of making life happen *for* me.

I was once that jet traveling well below 767 mph, allowing life to dictate what's ahead and what's to come. Not living up to my full potential was becoming an addictive habit. I was absorbing every negative blow life dealt and accepting the results with thoughts like, "Oh, there's a reason for everything; what doesn't kill me makes me stronger." That way of thinking is a coping mechanism that allows you to be more comfortable in mediocrity. Unfortunately, when you subconsciously agree with these statements, you become a resident of a hopeless community and environment. (I'll provide a short allegory on this place later.)

Furthermore, what doesn't kill you does precisely that: NOT KILL YOU! The statement should read more like this:

"What I don't allow to weaken me makes me stronger."

"What I won't allow to kill me keeps me alive longer."

You have decided to invest in yourself because you know deep down inside your core that there must be better, greater, and more to your life than what you have been experiencing.

One sole intention of mine for writing this book is to share these valuable tools and resources with you so that you can actively practice, participate in, activate, and apply them to make life happen *for* you

PREFACE: What is Vertical Living?

instead of *to* you. *You're Not High Enough* is packed with seven primary keys to wake up and unlock all the doors to your God-given potential.

In the Bible, James says, "Faith without works is dead," meaning that for God to activate what you want to happen in your life, *you first must participate*. I'll repeat it for the people in the back row…*for God to activate, you must participate!* We should, with maximum intensity, work to match our faith. We shouldn't move through life with all this hope but no strong will to see the plan through, maintain the mental edge, and apply maximum effort in our daily pursuits. You can't be 50/50 with the process; you must be all in 100% to make progress.

This is a huge barrier that, together, we will break from your life!

In the coming pages, you'll learn what I learned as I learned it, wrote it, and lived it. Then, finally, you will be given the keys to becoming a master craftsman—shaping and forming the life you want to live personally, professionally, spiritually, financially, and vertically.

These seven keys to living vertically will endow you with the power, principles, forward-thinking, wisdom, and ability to innovate, lead, and bless others. In addition, you'll develop the proper attributes needed to construct, form, and design an achievable blueprint that you can make into a reality … and that generations can build upon.

People ask me, "How did I write this book in 31 days?"

I tell them, "The writing was complete in 31 days, but it took me 20-plus years for the story to become a completed book."

I've always been the book from when I came out of Lorna Holt's womb at Miami Valley Hospital Sunday morning on October 16th in Dayton, OH. My experiences, failures, climbs, falls, fears, and doubts were countless pages for someone else to profit from, that someone being you.

So, if I'm a book, how much more are you a book with a story to tell that the world needs to read? We all are walking testimonies just bubbling with life, ready to spill over to help break barriers in one another's lives.

Taking time to ingest and then digest this material will awaken your senses to your inner greatness and your life's purpose and teach you how to transform yourself into an even more impactful individual who leads from the position of serving. I'm grateful that I desire to be more *impactful* than impressive. This book will encourage you along your journey to victory … even in what would seem like no-win situations. You'll develop the strength needed not just to begin the race of life but to thrive through the long middle stretch and continue to run firm throughout the race of life. As Tim S. Grover said in his best-selling book Winning, "Life is not a marathon; it is a race with no finish lines." Next time you hear someone say that life is a marathon, ask them when they last crossed the finish line. Why is such a statement so powerful to me? When are we ever indeed done running the race of life? Is life not more than just one total victory? Winning never stops, and neither does the race. Winning itself isn't handing out victories to everyone. There is a small select few it chooses. Those few who are selected are the best at continuously running with purpose and vision, never settling or becoming satisfied with just one victory. **True victory is outdoing yourself.** The race only ends when your life clock expires. So, while we have time, let us purposefully and intentionally run the race.

Stop chasing futile dreams and pursue profitable VISION.

Deep down, a giant field within you lacks the proper nutrients to develop and grow. The keys you'll discover in these pages will plant rich soil in your life, enabling you to produce a more significant crop than those weeds and thorns of problems and challenges that have been growing. In addition, you'll be taught how to recycle negativity into a positive renewable resource that will empower you to live vertically while gaining a spirit of excellence and personal success.

These teachings will add value to your skills and abilities, encourage you to evolve into a better you, and bless you as you transform into

PREFACE: What is Vertical Living?

an elite VISIONARY. You'll learn to be a "doer, " not just a hearer and thinker. You will hunger to EXECUTE. You will find completeness in consistency and progress in persistence. Your mind will be rehabbed and cleansed of a culturally influenced, conditioned, and impoverished mindset. Finally, you will discover how a framework of reasonable effort will reward you in total EFFICIENCY.

You're Not High Enough will instill life-changing concepts and fresh ideas into your life. The potential to refashion and remodel your existence will allow you to learn how to effectively destroy anything contrary to you, living vertically, becoming a visionary, and fulfilling the purposeful mission God has ordained for you each day. Life is a moment-by-moment experience… *don't rush God's process; trust God's process.* Or if that's not your thing, begin to trust in more progress than process. If this is a new concept to you or you've forgotten, God's timing is always on time.

You're Not High Enough will birth more extraordinary fathers and mothers, diligent people in business, impeccable global leaders, improved thinkers, and a generation of high character, high integrity, and highly intellectual individuals.

If you're stuck at one speed and in desperate need of a boost to break that sound barrier in your life to impact the lives of others, *You're Not High Enough* is the boost you've been longing for.

This book will strengthen and encourage you, increase your self-value and worth, and help you learn to yield the highest return on your greater investment of self. To be a great investor, you must first thoroughly understand the investment and thus become the investment. It is an honor to begin investing in you while on your journey!

> ARE YOU READY TO LEVEL UP?
> ARE YOU READY TO SOAR?
> ARE YOU READY TO GO VERTICAL?
> ARE YOU READY TO BIRTH VISION?

KEY I:
VISIONARY or Dreamer?

> *Then the Lord answered me and said,*
> *"Record the vision and inscribe it on tablets,*
> *That the one who reads it may run.*
> *For the vision is yet for the appointed time.*
>
> *It hastens toward the goal, and it will not fail.*
>
> *Though it tarries, wait for it;*
> *For it will certainly come, it will not delay."*
> (Habakkuk 2:2-3)

Are you a dreamer or a VISIONARY?

Do you know what both terms mean for your life?

Before you answer either question, let me introduce this chapter by informing you of the importance of doing away with futile dreams and incorporating purposeful vision. Why would I encourage you to put a stop to big dreaming? You're probably thinking, "I'm supposed to dream big, right?" I would submit no because that's what you've been taught all your life.

Has anyone ever taught you how to effectively and appropriately make those dreams come true? How many people, institutions, or organizations—that push for dreaming big—ever handed you the keys to unlock the door to your biggest dreams? Even more, how many of those big dreams have ever come true?

Take a minute. I'll patiently wait.

Rest assured, I'll explain in this chapter—and throughout this book—why your dreams must die and your vision must come alive. It will save you from further damaging yourself by wasting time. It's to your advantage that you eliminate this idea of pushing toward accomplishing a dream. This could be a blessing you've been waiting on, seeing that no one else who kept telling you to "dream big" cared enough or knew how to guide you to do it.

By removing the illusion of what you believe is dreams, the conception of a purposed vision can be birthed into your life! As you continue reading these pages, the seeds planted will grow and give you a more clear and complete vision.

Now, quickly locate a mirror and say aloud, with the most conviction you can muster, "I am no longer a dreamer but now a VISIONARY."

> **"Nothing comes to a dreamer but more sleep and more dreams."**

So, what is a dreamer? Instead of sharing what Webster defines and what you already know yourself, allow me to give my definition as it first applies to the subject matter: *A dreamer is a person who is naive to reality and never does what is required; a dreamer lies in a dormant and stagnant state of being while consciously chasing a false reality.*

Do you remember the classic movie *The Matrix*? There was a particular scene when Morpheus, Neo's mentor, presented two pills to Neo: one red and one blue. Morpheus explained that everything Neo had ever believed and seen was a lie that the system had generated. People were asleep in these gooey-filled pods, being kept alive by machines transmitting a false reality of their world.

KEY I: VISIONARY or Dreamer?

The machines were harvesting the humans like cattle, feeding off humanity's life source—energy—to sustain their existence. Their false vision of reality fueled and drove the machines to continue to have power over the humans as they slept and kept dreaming, thus keeping them bound to the pods and, ultimately, the machines. That vision was clearly made a reality, keeping humans in a dream state. As long as humans stayed dreaming, unaware of being controlled and entertained by a false reality, the machines would always remain in control.

I would compare a dreamer to those stuck in "The Matrix"—asleep, unconscious to reality, and unaware of their true potential. When people ask themselves *why is this happening to me?* It is a clear sign that you may be what keeps happening to you at some point. Unfortunately, many dreamers aren't cognizant that they are experiencing a reality setup for them to be more followers than leaders. More consumers than producers. More spenders than earners. There are more complainers than those who compliment. Dreamers wait for things to happen instead of making things happen. As a result, the world comprises two types of people: Those who do and those who won't.

Are you chasing life in vain? Could you be chasing regret, not even knowing it? Have you been dreaming of a fulfilled purpose so long that you have grown numb to what that even takes and feels like to make happen?

If you answered yes, maybe, or I don't know to those questions, allow my next question to compel you to think even more critically:

How many dreams have you set for yourself, your life, and your future that have fully come to pass?

I don't want you to confuse goals, purpose, and potential with dreams. But, also, let's use our common sense that when I refer to dreams or dreaming, I'm not defining it as the type that comes by way of sleep.

Think about all the dreams you've waited for to happen in real-time; how close have you come to experiencing them fully? As you think about this, allow me to share some additional imagery of what a dreamer is:

A dreamer could be compared to a thick, swelling cloud of water hovering above the earth. Everyone below sees it, expecting rain, yet the cloud never produces a single drop.

The world consists of all types of dreamers who are like clouds floating about life with the appearance of great potential, yet the world will never witness any of this potential nor observe it come to fruition. My point is that dreamers, sadly, never produce any results!

The grave has amassed generations of dead men's thoughts, concepts, ideas, and intentional plans. Notice I didn't mention dreams, and for a good reason. Here's a short list of dead men who didn't dream but instead had a vision that impacted the world: Alexander Hamilton, Walt Disney, Carnegie Steele, Christiana Carteaux Bannister, Henry Ford, Martin Luther King Jr., Steve Jobs, Kobe Bryant (2020 RIP Bean), Thomas L. Jennings, and the list goes on. You might have to Google a few names on this list to know who they are, but each was an extraordinary visionary… not a dreamer. Although buried and long gone, their vision is still alive, active, and impacting your world today.

True vision, no matter how big or small, never succumbs to death. The cemetery, unfortunately, has a high population of dreamers whose dreams followed them right to the grave.

Dreams don't come true; opportunities do

I spent much of my life as a dreamer, and the time spent dreaming cost me millions. I may not have physically lost millions of dollars, but dreaming did cost me millions in minutes, hours, and days wasted.

How much of your time and money has been wasted on vain pursuits? If you've been counting on dreams, you've been counting yourself out.

KEY I: VISIONARY or Dreamer?

You might have noticed that I ask many questions. This is so that I can engage with your mind. I ask questions because I want to encourage you to think from a Socratic approach so that you can process intelligently and make the best-informed decision from yourself as to why you must wake up from your slumber of false dream living.

After you've breathed the life-giving oxygen of this opening key, breathing in the truth about yourself, you will be empowered to apply these keys as practical applications, creating a pathway toward your vision of completion and vertical living.

Speaking of dreams, have you ever considered what the "American Dream" really is—what it should look like, how it should feel, and even what it should taste like? Of course, television, media, and culture have shaped many ideas of what it is, but have you honestly asked yourself, "Do I possess what it takes to live the American Dream?"

Take a minute to self-reflect on those questions.

The "American Dream" is one gigantic false lullaby to which almost everyone has fallen asleep. Nevertheless, the American Dream has spread its hopes globally because every country, nation, and province has its separate form of the American Dream. This is based on the ideology of life, liberty, and the pursuit of happiness. This concept is the very fabric of why an individual desires to pursue the American Dream due to the desire to experience better opportunities in America.

The American Dream is not lived by those who chase dreams. The American Dream is not enjoyed by those who are only talkers. That two-story mansion in Nantucket, hidden in a gated community with a $100K foreign vehicle parked out front, is not awarded to those who dream, stop running and don't have a vision.

The Fortune 500 company you admire that generates hundreds of millions of dollars in annual revenue was not erected by individuals who just lived their lives chasing dreams. Likewise, your favorite actor or musician didn't become your favorite by only dreaming about being famous. Much thought, discipline, and work were put in so that a plan and executable vision would create an opportunity for themselves.

Who is the type of person that creates this life for themselves? What kind of person enjoys life by impacting it? Who possesses the intensity to make life bend and the willpower for life to do whatever they create?

This type of person living life vertically is called a "VISIONARY."

My definition of a VISIONARY has three meanings:

1. An individual who sees a problem and believes without fear or doubt that they have the know-how, willpower, and skill to provide a solution.
2. An individual who possesses a unique gift and talent that will stop at nothing to make their vision a reality not only in their own life but will see it come to pass in the lives of others.
3. An individual who figures it out.

Today, that's YOU!

Today, you're embarking on breaking the sound barrier of life and becoming an unstoppable force of creativity, innovation, and brilliance. Today, you realize that you've been asleep long enough.

Are you ready to IMPACT the world and not just make an impression? You can do and become anything you want in this life. You have the God-given ability to shape and change matter just as much as Blake Mycoskie or S. Truett Cathy—creators of Toms Shoes and Chick-fil-A, respectively, did. So why mention these two men above other greats? If you haven't noticed, I'm a man of faith and drawn to other men of faith.

Blake and Truett were high men of faith who desired to impact the world, not just impress it. They chose to live vertically and wanted others to soar with them. They decided that their business and creative practices would be worked to God's glory and display a characteristic of who God is in their lives and products. *I admire that they upheld* **PEOPLE** *over profit and* **INTEGRITY** *over income.* Having a vision and experiencing its positive results is not for yourself alone but for others also. That's what it's all about—living life for others to do well. People will forever always be the most significant and most valuable commodity.

Do nothing from selfishness or empty conceit, but with humility, regard one another as more important than yourselves.
Philippians 2:3 (NASB)

I hope one of the many takeaways you receive from this book and your desire to birth a vision will include more than just becoming rich, famous, and overly successful. This book was not intended for you to follow a formula to become wealthy or use this information to sell more products like other self-help books promote. Instead, I want you to become an improved, upgraded version of yourself: a better citizen, a more people-conscious business owner, a more mentally sharp athlete, a more present father, and a woman who has added more value and self-worth for herself. In addition, I want you to improve your thoughts and become more aware of why you believe what you think.

I aim for these seven keys to give you an advantage in approaching problems. I want to help you understand why it's better to stop dealing with problems and have the mindset to overcome problems with solutions. When you say that you're "tired of dealing with this" or "I'm just going have to deal with it," you are internally saying that I don't mind tolerating what gives me high anxiety, stress, and grief. Stop dealing and do more overcoming. One perspective that helped me immensely was when I learned to compartmentalize my emotions to become powerfully more logical in my actions and decision-making. Earlier, I said that the best investor is the one who fully understands the investment itself. When I cut out being so emotionally invested in situations, expectations of people, outcomes, and problems, it was then that I became a better investor. I began to remove my attempts to control things, people, circumstances, and situations over which I had no power. I became more aware of where I invested my attention, time, creativity, focus, and energy. As a result, the return on my investment led to more peace, productivity, and prosperity.

I desire that you become more aware of the greatness that God has placed inside you so that you hopefully learn to love God more fully, appropriately love yourself more, and love your neighbor even more as yourself. I also hope you become encouraged by noticing how following the examples taught by Jesus Christ changed my life and blessed me with much added and needed wisdom to write this book … and that the same can happen to you.

Below are three powerful tools a dreamer must use to break through life's barriers to living vertically. These three concepts, once applied, will undoubtedly produce massive gains in your life, driving you toward your passion and joy-fulfilled living:

> *1) A REPROGRAMMED MIND*
> *2) ABILITY TO HYPER-SEE*
> *3) MAKING FEAR YOUR TAILWIND*

The Reprogrammed Mind

*"… and have put on the **new self** who is being **renewed** to a true **knowledge** according to the **image** of the One who created him …"*
(Colossians 3:10 NASB)

The very first step in becoming a VISIONARY is to take back the rich mind God gave you. The enslaved mind must be free from what you

KEY I: VISIONARY or Dreamer?

have been taught, trained, and conditioned to believe early in life. Unfortunately, this also includes destructive habits that have set up shop in your mind and life.

You've been allowed to believe it's okay to look like what you're going through. Next, you were instructed not to change your environment but to let your environment change you. Lastly, you were taught to be an employee rather than an employer in every aspect of your everyday life.

The first key to reprogramming the mind is by way of a lifestyle change. Therefore, it would help if you committed to a new way of living, thinking, and appropriately feeling.

Many people desperately avoid committing to new commitments due to a pre-conditioned, impaired, and dysfunctional way of living. Throughout much of my life, and having had many toxic habits, I've realized that we tend to be lazy ... and lazy people generally despise learning, applying, acting on, and utilizing knowledge and wisdom. The perspective of lazy-minded people is that they always have ample time to continue to put off.

"The [reverent] fear of the Lord [that is, worshiping Him and regarding Him as truly awesome] is the beginning and the preeminent part of <u>knowledge</u> [its starting point and its essence]; but arrogant [a]fools despise [skillful and godly] wisdom and instruction and self-discipline." (Proverbs 1:7 AMP)

"My people are destroyed for lack of knowledge."
(Hosea 4:6 NKJV)

I don't fully believe the mind is the controlling force of actions of the body. There's not enough attention given to our hearts for being the "brains" of operations and instructions that are carried out (this is neither scientifically proven as well). From an emotional perspective, I believe we were created with a conscious and subconscious mind, and our soul makes up the conscious part of our feelings, thoughts, and mind—narrative.

Now, the subconscious is the center of your being; this makes you who you are; it is your very nature. In this case, your heart is your subconscious, not the physical heart, whose main job is to pump and distribute blood. Your heart—the center of being—initiates and brings to life every thought, concept, and idea the mind carries out.

Whatever you believe and speak from the heart shows the type of person you are and what you are made of. The words spoken out of the mouth are birthed from the heart, which frames, dictates, and sets the course of your life.

> *"For as he thinks in his heart, so is he."*
> **(Proverbs 23:7 NASB)**

If you only talk about what you would like to do and what you're going to do, but all you produce are words and not actions, then you're a dreamer. If you've never put valuable time, commitment, and dedication into what you talk about, then you have a lazy heart and no work ethic. This is also a sign that you don't believe in yourself or the words you speak about yourself… *without true belief, there is no real action.*

The most common reason dreamers talk about different projects and goals but never accomplish them is that they lack a sound heart, willpower, and a "4th quarter" mentality. This type of person has a dream but not a plan. And even with a plan, they never continue to check off small objectives so that the plan would continue to evolve. Now, having a lazy heart mixed with a negative conformed mind with no strategic purpose, one will continually be indecisive and almost always deviating. Without a plan, preparation can't exist. The slacker believes that tomorrow is promised to them, so there is no sense of

KEY I: VISIONARY or Dreamer?

urgency to handle business for the day at hand. I've had multiple turning points that have shifted my focus and sense of urgency to improve. I came to the notion from experiencing numerous deaths in my family that tomorrow is promised; it's just not guaranteed to me. That, with much conviction, reshaped a great deal of my perspective on life. From that moment, a conviction set in, and time was no longer anything to waste anymore. Time became the gold standard of my life!

Another area of demise for a dreamer is what they negatively speak from the heart. A person believes and becomes what they speak. Ralph Waldo Emmerson said best: *"A man is what he thinks about all day long."* If you have negative *"I can't"* thoughts, these silent words are formed in your subconscious before becoming a concept. Once this pessimistic, lazy, defeated vision is crystalized, it becomes an idea. After your thought becomes an idea, it then transforms into a reality. When individuals say, *"I wish,"* they're eliminating themselves from contention to make it happen. When you're always saying, *"I'll try,"* you're leaving a high chance that you won't.

I can attest from my own life that what you think and speak is a universal and spiritual law. Therefore, it is best to purposely say life-giving affirmations to live and experience the vertical part of life. A VISIONARY must have full access to this way of thinking and knowledge to impact the world with a vision.

> *"Death and life are in the power of the tongue,*
> *And those who love it will eat its fruit."*
> **(Proverbs 18:21 NASB)**

Aimless dream chasing never ends and constantly changes. This will be true in all the projects, goals, and tasks that a dreamer begins construction on but never completes. When the mind has not been appropriately reprogrammed and realigned, the dreamer is always in a "start and stop" loop—always starting a new dream only to stop and then move on to another one because they didn't have the endurance, knowledge, perseverance, and discipline to carry out the first of many other dreams. This also stems from what I stated earlier as intense dream chasing. Seeing that there is no pursuit, the goal can only be within reach and obtainable for so long before it's no longer visible. So many factors can make the visibility of chasing dreams blurry.

> **What are some areas in your life causing you to chase and not pursue?**

Once frustration sets in, the mind and heart become discouraged because no fruit is being produced due to being a dreamer. Seeing that there is no fruit from the laboring of futile dream chasing coupled with no vision, the individual will seek out a new dream, hoping to achieve the results they wanted from the previously failed dream. Some would confuse this as "figuring it out." I would label it as insanity. They are looking for different and new results by doing the same thing repeatedly. This cycle can last for years if one is not careful and observant of the toxic tendency.

> *You must stop dreaming and start envisioning.*

Envisioning emphasizes planning; planning creates structure, and structure builds the foundation. These are vital components that lead to the production of sustainable results.

There must be an end put to a lazy mind for reprogramming to take place. My failed dreams, lazy heart, and convoluted mind awarded me ten months of homelessness in 2014. I realized that none of my big dreams helped me avoid living in the basement of a church and out of the trunk of my 2013 Chevy Impala. Drawing back on that, I'm

KEY I: VISIONARY or Dreamer?

embarrassed to say I only made one payment on the car. That alone confirms my way of living and thinking was ill. More than anything, this was due to making a dumb decision to purchase a car I couldn't afford. As I recall those painful moments, I never knew how much I was dreaming until the reality of the consequences woke me up. If you've ever found yourself in a negative situation and at that point asking, "How did I get here?" Rest assured, you've finally woken up. These consequences are now ready to collect on the debts of poor decision-making.

I would compare a dreamer to an overly intoxicated person. You know that you've been drinking, but it's once impaired; you're unaware of what you're doing and how your decisions are increasingly becoming detrimental to your life by the very second. It's not until the following day that the consequences begin to show up for what you've done. Therefore, your thoughts, behaviors, and habits must remain sober. I would preach to my kids in 7th grade that their vision for themselves now and the patterns they practice today will dictate their quality of life when they reach their thirties. I would do my best to drill this perspective into their mindset. However, the way you practice is how you will perform. I always taught them that practice doesn't make perfect; practice makes the performance, and if you can perfect your practice, that practice will become permanent.

It's a straightforward algorithm. *If* you don't practice the importance and discipline of making your bed now, *then* you won't be as successful and reach your full potential—simple Algorithm. There is so much to learn from routinely and consistently making your bed. It's not so much the bedmaking part that's most important here… it's the mindset behind making your bed that should hit home. If you can't develop the discipline to make your bed, you'll approach every part of life that requires this practiced discipline the same way. A poor mindset brings about an impoverished lifestyle. I view life in levels when it comes to specific practices and disciplines. If I can't consistently show up to properly make my bed every morning, that same approach and mindset will show up for me every day of life, especially when it matters the most. A messy bed, messy life is the thought here.

How badly do you want to thrive in life?

If you can't be dedicated and a high performer in the simple tasks of life, how can you excel and be consistent in the primary next-level functions of life?

If you don't have a vision and never reprogram your mind early in life, how much worse will it be later?

At that time, I had been in a false state of dreaming for about ten years when I finally woke up broke, homeless, in debt, without a plan, and with no vision. I was blind to my actions, digging a ditch so deep that it would require three shovels to get myself out. When I finally looked up and saw how far I was from the top, I knew I had dug a severe hole in my life. Being a lazy-hearted dreamer led to sorting through a trunk full of clothes and occasionally taking wash-ups in public restrooms. That was the type of reality my dreaming led to!

There must be a **FED-UP** *moment!*

When drastic action is needed, drastic changes must be made. Being completely honest with yourself and admitting that YOU are the reason the hole has become a crater is the first and most crucial step to recovery. Then, there must be a firm conviction of WHY for the changes needed. I found that my kids would be my greatest why. Having this mind shift is what significantly led to the process of reprogramming my mind for a better, more promising tomorrow. I began committing to behavioral changes that went against my muddy reality, lazy heart, and mind. I stop lying to myself. I quit making excuses. I became more proactive and began to fall in love with the results.

KEY I: VISIONARY or Dreamer?

> *A humbling reality needed for your growth is recognizing that your method hasn't worked all your life.*

Knowledge is only powerful if practically applied to your life. Knowledge will grant you access to the keys, unlocking many doors of opportunities. This process begins by learning from others who have tested and experienced the level of living you desire. One bit of wisdom I tell aspiring millionaires is that your first million is made by obtaining knowledge and reading insightful material religiously.

Of course, your checking account won't instantly have millions of dollars, but you will begin to set a tone and create a vision that can lead you to millions over time.

I can't stress enough that your first investment—the one that will yield you the most excellent ROI (Return on Investment)—is desperately seeking and obtaining appropriate knowledge... knowledge that is a model you can build on. Every expert, author, and speaker is not for you. Often, it's best to be surgical with knowledge, cut out the parts that don't benefit you, and keep the pieces that will improve your life. Keep in mind that not all knowledge is beneficial knowledge all the time. Reading can be challenging, especially if you've developed a habit and mindset to live without it. So, seeing that reading was an area in my life that was lacking, I began to read material that was modeled for me. This was a lazy addiction that wasn't so hard to kick. I believe it won't be for you either, especially if you're at a point in life where you know real change is vital.

The first book I seriously read from an application point of view was *Secrets of The Millionaire Mind* by T. Harv Eker (thank you, TZ, for recommending this read to me years ago). This book introduced activating a reprogrammed mind financially, personally, and professionally. I quickly became a student of finance. I learned from T. Harv that to become a VISIONARY and make millions of dollars to bless the world, I would first have to correct my financial blueprint. I had to readjust my thoughts, attitudes, and behavior toward money. How I was raised and conditioned to view money had to be wiped entirely from the hard drive of my mind. The way I witnessed my parents grinding and toiling, going into debt for my sister and me to enjoy Christmas and birthdays year after year, was setting me on a course toward financial doom.

The way I was unconsciously taught to work only to spend money and not to save and invest money had to be eradicated from my way of life financially. Furthermore, how I handled money and even what I spoke about money had to be revamped and corrected in my daily language.

For example, I could no longer plan to save money "for a rainy day" because if I talked about it and believed it, a rainy day would surely come. How dreadful a feeling when you've saved a nice chunk of change only to witness it vanish for a "rainy day." I like to be prepared for unexpected events, not save all my money to blow from a costly mistake. This, in my opinion, is saving for a rainy day.

Secrets of the Millionaire Mind taught me how to perform and play to win, not play to defend so that I don't lose. That mentality will minimize your aggression, allowing much comfort and room to be passive. When you're overthinking, it increases the chances for mistakes to be made, costing you the game. I was developing a new attitude to investing so that my money would work for me instead of overworking for it. While reading *Secrets of the Millionaire Mind*, and for a while afterward, I underwent a massive overhaul and dumping of toxic ideology, concepts, and practices. How you view money, the rich, and anything about money is critical to how you receive and utilize money. Ask yourself these questions when you loosely say you'll be a millionaire.

> *Why do you want to become a millionaire?*
> *What will it cost for you to become a millionaire?*

KEY I: VISIONARY or Dreamer?

> *What happens when you get the first million?*
> *How will you keep up doing what it took*
> *to make another million?*

These questions must be asked, and you must take them seriously in all pursuits of vertical living. So many people say what they want but never mean it because they're unwilling to pay the price it will cost to become a reality. Making a conscious effort to ask yourself the right questions for your life sets the course for you to create and have an intense action plan for your success.

It was no easy feat when I admitted myself into financial rehab; I was both knees deep in debt. My credit score was so bad that I forgot I had one! I only saved money to spend money, and I wasted even what I didn't have. I began to ponder deeply why I believe I'd want to receive and handle a million dollars when I was finding it difficult to manage $1,000. Desiring how to be faithful over a little so that you become great over much is a learned practice that takes time to develop.

I believe the two main reasons people labor in efforts to become wealthy and struggle while doing it are the following:

1. IMPOVERISHED PLANNING.
2. A LACK OF WILLINGNESS TO GAIN KNOWLEDGE.

It's not that people don't want knowledge or that knowledge is scarce. It boils down to the fact that most people have no desire to pursue and commit to knowledge actively and fully. For example, in the book of Proverbs—one of my favorites in the Bible—there's a scripture where the writer exclaims that wisdom cries out in the open market and the streets for any who passes by to come to receive! But day after day, no one turns in to acquire this wisdom because they have no desire; it's not a part of their life plan to-do list.

Regrettably, the ones you'll find passing by are the naïve, the broke, and above all, THE DREAMERS!

> *"Learn to stop taking the easy to start taking the ACCURATE."*
> —Dr. Myles Munroe

Everything I had been taught about money, working a job, and exchanging time for income had to be destroyed from the deepest part of my brain and heart. My financial blueprint was horrendous, and it would stay that way indefinitely at my current pace. While reading the book, it dawned on me that my current state of mind financially was so distorted that if I stayed on that path of thinking, I would be in poverty forever. Yes, I would have many jobs and see steady wage increases, but I was never getting ahead because I was doing things like creating more debt to pay for bad expenses, e.g., jewelry, fashion, Jordans, etc. It's worth mentioning that jobs aren't designed to make you rich, and I would suggest striving to become independent of them.

Instead of creating autonomous trends, I was following them. T. Harv's book corrected many errors in how I looked at and spent money. *Secrets of the Millionaire Mind* did more than enhance my financial knowledge; it gave me something far more valuable. It made me aware that I didn't understand how money and finances worked. In life, it's never an abundance issue but an awareness issue that causes many to stay in poverty.

Consequently, in a powerful, transforming way, I was enlightened to how much greater I could become. After completing the book and practicing what I learned and what was fed into my heart, I felt empowered; I felt like I had achieved something unique by being disciplined and completing one book. I felt wealthy because I was now rich in knowledge. I learned that with the right motive and a reprogrammed mind, I was on to something that would save my life and that of my children.

After reading the book, my most significant piece of wisdom came by asking myself a serious question and one that may move you: How would it have ever been possible for me to earn a million dollars when I didn't even know how to invest in myself?

> **"Change your heart in the right way to experience a life rightly lived."**

The heart and mind should be a team, but all too often, the heart leads the mind on unwise paths. If the heart is offbeat, the mind won't be in sync. I believe the mind only agrees with what the heart speaks. The role your mind plays is to project a visual. That could be something negative or positive, depending on the desire warranted.

For example, think of something as simple as knowing that the relationship you're in is non-beneficial. Even though your mind has made perfect sense of why you should leave (logical), your heart has convinced your mind you should stay (emotional). You realize you shouldn't have followed your heart only after heartache and heartbreak have transpired. Having a strong sense of reasoning can sort out what makes sense and what doesn't. The heart only pursues what the heart wants.

Following the heart is not necessarily bad; it only becomes harmful when it is offbeat. Offbeat in wisdom, discipline, faith, and knowledge.

Becoming a visionary and reaching vertical living is like going to the gym to transform your body; you must work it and push it to uncomfortable levels. Yet, you often progress most during life's strenuous and challenging times! Everything in your life most assuredly becomes a reality according to your faith. In other words, whatever vision God has granted you to conceive becomes a reality, depending on where your heart and faith lie.

If you say, "I'm just hanging in there, that is according to your faith, and every part of your life will always reflect those results of just hanging in there. If you find yourself saying, "I'll never get that promotion," or "I don't have the time to read on how to invest and save," when those anticipated moments consistently don't happen for you, please don't think it strange or question, "Why me? Why is this not happening? How come I'm never able to save? Why am I always without money? My boss doesn't like me, why? This company sucks! I hate my body! I'll never have that! It'll take too long before I can do the impossible!"

So much faith was activated in those loose, negative words that you didn't even realize you were living precisely what you've been speaking and believing. So, listen, my friend, you must repeatedly hammer this into your senses, reprogramming the heart and the mind so that it sinks in and is deposited into your soul:

You'll never have VISION or become a VISIONARY unless what you have previously read up until now becomes as natural as breathing air in your lungs.

Studies suggest that it takes 21 days for a fundamental habit to take effect. In my own life, I can attest to this. I desperately wanted to create a new habit and routine but didn't know where to begin. One example occurred when my church had 21 days of prayer. We would meet at 7 am and have brief worship to some praise music, a 10-to-15-minute devotional, then break for individual prayer for about 30-35 minutes, and lastly, come together in prayer for 5-10 minutes to end. This was precisely what I needed to start creating a new habit and discipline myself to get to bed. This unique preparation would allow me to get adequate rest so that waking up at 6 a.m. would not be a struggle. I would have to prepare diligently so I would not make it on time but arrive early. This helped me become more aware of how I utilized my time for the day. I was eating breakfast again because I wasn't sleeping until late afternoon. I felt purpose in the morning because it started with connecting with God and others for an hour, creating a positive start to my day. In addition, I was now able to get back in the gym, which I had been putting off for months, and now, with this new routine, I began to see a mental and physical transformation.

There's a saying, "Garbage in, garbage out." If you involve yourself with trash long enough, you'll eventually be on the curb waiting to be picked up and dumped. The same goes for the type of company you keep as well. If you hang with trash, your life will always reflect that unless you change how you think and wisely rearrange your sphere of influence and the company you keep. As Scripture tells us, "Do not be deceived: Bad company corrupts good morals" (1 Corinthians 15:33 NASB). If you desire to create and live the VISION you believe for your life, you'll need to cut out 100% of the garbage stinking up your life and robbing you of the blessings God has planned for you.

> "It was when I started to CUT the ROPES of the FOLKS, I was HANGING with that I began to SEE clearly." —Wavie Lee

No one should ever feel comfortable with life just picking them up and dumping them out repeatedly. Instead, create a new habit for 21 days of filling your life with positive affirmations. On top of that, shut off the idiot box (TV), tell social media you're breaking up for three weeks, and only do things that will elevate your focus. I also recommend—not a command—establishing a more concrete relationship with God; there's no harm in picking up the Bible and getting acquainted with God's character.

If you are new to the Bible, have never read it, or have grown frustrated that you don't get it, then I suggest reading through the book of Proverbs. It speaks of wisdom, knowledge, and understanding. Then, I encourage you to download a Bible app to read different translations if you have a smartphone, tablet, or any device that connects to the

Internet. In my opinion, the New Living Translation (NLT) is the most straightforward translation for beginners. Many Bible apps exist, but my favorite is the YouVersion Bible app. They have a ton of FREE content, interactive, engaging material, and easy-to-follow devotionals that will help you stay focused, mentally sharp, and attentively active during your 21 days of reprogramming. My suggestion if this is an option for you would be to follow through because YOU want to and not because I said so. If you believe there is some real value in making the effort that can come about, then let it work for you. Never let the opinions and judgments of others sway you into doing or not doing what you should do.

If discovering God's Word can add to your life, incorporate it into your likes, gifts, passions, and skills! If you like to draw, write, or create, grab some material to enhance those skills. Take the time to learn a little about a lot of things.

Notice how I mentioned, "learn a little." A true VISIONARY knows a little about many things. This is a great weapon to have at your disposal so that you become more than one-dimensional, allowing you to add more value to the lives of those you're impacting, including yourself. Learning about other topics, subjects, and crafts will grant you access to doors you never knew existed. Trust me, you will become such an expert that people will pay you for the knowledge that's always been free.

Why would a person pay you for free knowledge that they could receive independently? The answer is simple: the person who pays for the expert knowledge of someone else is either lazy or is okay with not being self-sufficient. Let's be honest: I didn't just come out of the womb with this knowledge—this way of thinking and living. It took time; I had to endure a lot, but I also had a burning desire to improve myself while serving others. That also included obtaining and retaining new knowledge.

I've only made it this far with God and Him helping me REPROGRAM my mind. You will, too!

KEY I: VISIONARY or Dreamer?

Begin to Hyper-See

Visionaries have an uncanny ability to "Hyper-See." Having a reprogrammed mind unleashes your full potential and power to unlock this much-needed VISIONARY attribute. Does Gutzon Borglum sound familiar to you? If not, I recommend you research and familiarize yourself with him. Gutzon Borglum was the mastermind, master craftsman, and creator of the historic Mount Rushmore, along with many other ingenious works of art.

The fantastic imagery of Mount Rushmore today is different from how it looked before its completion some 70 years ago. When looking intently at Mount Rushmore, would you believe its beginning was nothing but desolate stones with no future? Mr. Borglum, on the other hand, saw something far more than just granite and rocks. He was able to HYPER-SEE the entire project completion before creating a blueprint, picking up a tool, and setting a date for construction.

I believe Mr. Borglum had pre-envisioned that area with great potential, allowing him to transform it into a masterful patriotic structure of American history. Based on the results, it's easy to assert that Gutzon visualized it before ever starting it. This is too Hyper-See. He believed it before seeing it, which is what a VISIONARY must do above all else. You must know that what doesn't exist *does* exist before ever seeing its existence. Mr. Borglum envisioned solutions and saw the successful outcome before any outside doubt or fear could arise.

> *"I have made you a father of many nations in the sight of Him in whom he believed, that is, God who gives life to the dead and <u>calls into being that which does not exist</u>."* (Romans 4:17 AMP)

So, you're probably wondering how I was introduced to this concept. First, let me briefly explain what it means to Hyper-See. To Hyper-See is a belief, just as well as a mindset. Hyper-seeing is the ability to have an intense focus visualizing the completion of a desire yet to become.

Here's a small example: you decided you wanted pizza for lunch well before lunchtime. You first thought it; you then believed that's what you were eating, and then you decided that your favorite pizza spot would make having lunch a real thing. Hyper-seeing falls along the lines of believing in something that hasn't yet become a reality. It is your thoughts that activate your words.

It is this understanding that what you desire and believe in will become something real before having it, tasting it, or physically seeing it. This is a proper lens a visionary sees through. The ability to Hyper-See is profound—as I'll explain later—through the eyes of Jesus.

Hyper-seeing eliminates all doubt; it cancels out what can't happen and what is considered impossible, enabling it to become possible. Hyper-seeing takes great faith based on an even greater hope. Whomever Hyper-Sees believes they can turn "not enough" into "a whole lot."

> **BELIEVE IT. SEE IT. BECOME IT.**

An essential ingredient behind the ability to Hyper-See is ACTION! Without action, there are no results. You can have all the faith, say all the affirmations, and believe until you're convinced, but without action, there is no fulfilled desire.

The revelation of the term Hyper-See emerged during a run of biblical and motivational videos I uploaded to YouTube in 2014. While reading God's Word, I encountered one of Jesus' many great miracles: feeding five thousand men, not including women and children, with five barley loaves and two fish. In this story, a small portion of the scripture would be a goldmine to my perspective, leading to the miraculous feat that only ...

> *a) Christ The Lord could perform, and*
> *b) only a VISIONARY with the ability to Hyper-See can manifest true desires into reality.*

KEY I: VISIONARY or Dreamer?

Before I go further, I must be clear that I am considerate and mindful of my readers' religious beliefs and views. I do not use my faith and relationship with Christ to sway or influence you into sharing the same belief as me. I use the term "relationship" because I don't consider myself religious. If I were indeed a religious individual with all its customs, rules, biases, hypocrisy, and traditions, I would not have been able to write this book with such inner truth, transparency, passion, selflessness, conviction, and emotion. My point of emphasis in illustrating this story of Jesus is to show and amplify that VISIONARIES, which Jesus was, can perform more extraordinary feats and execute at higher levels than dreamers. That said, allow me to point out the scriptures I was referring to:

Now the day was ending, and the twelve came and said to Him, "Send the crowd away, that they may go into the surrounding villages and countryside and find lodging and get something to eat; for here we are in a desolate place."

But He told them, "You give them something to eat!"

And they said, "We have no more than five loaves and two fish unless perhaps we go and buy food for all these people." (For there were about five thousand men.)

And He said to His disciples, "Have them sit down to eat in groups of about fifty each." They did so and had them all sit-down. Then He took the five loaves and the two fish, and looking up to heaven, He blessed them, and broke them, and kept giving them to the disciples to set before the people. And they all ate and were satisfied, and the broken pieces which they had left over were picked up, twelve baskets full. (Luke 9:10-17 NASB)

This passage of scripture relates to a VISIONARY being able to Hyper-See while a dreamer only has limited natural vision. Natural vision allows you to see things precisely as they are (often worse than what they are). The disciples' vision only allowed them to see the conditions as they were: lack, bareness, and not enough. At the same time, Christ saw the complete opposite. Our greatest VISIONARY saw more than enough; He saw provision; His calculations added to abundance and an eventually fed and satisfied crowd. This is one of many experiences of vertical living. You are rising above your situation to look down at the problems that attempt to pull you down. When living vertically, you never become lower than the problem or circumstance. Instead, you set the bar high enough that the problem must reach your level to affect your progress.

Visionaries can analyze and innovate any situation, providing a resolution far greater than the problem suggests. Unfortunately, many people today are exactly like the disciples were during the days of Jesus. Most people can't even reach their maximum potential because they limit themselves by what they see in front of them. These dreamers only wish to bring change, impact a culture, or live through someone else's vision.

> **"The farmer never buries a seed;
> the farmer always plants a VISION."**

The disciples' minuscule level of faith and vision is apparent in the scripture. Still, we see Jesus as a true VISIONARY with a maximum ability to Hyper-See. In the disciples' defense, they were still in training and not yet genuinely comprehending what was occurring before their eyes in the company of Jesus.

There was a moment in the story when Christ even offered them to see through the same heighted lens as He looked through by telling the disciples, "You give them something to eat" (verse 13).

KEY I: VISIONARY or Dreamer?

In my opinion, this was a clear giveaway that the disciples were also endowed with the same ability to perform the same miracle(s) that Christ did, only they didn't know it initially. But on that day, among the crowds of five thousand, when Christ displayed and established faith and belief, the disciples showed an even greater level of ambiguity and skepticism.

If Christ hadn't granted them this same power, He would not have told the disciples to feed the hungry crowd. I'm sure there have been moments when you didn't recognize your ability, gift, high level of thinking, great idea, or unique talent. I'm sure there's been a time you couldn't see that you could erect change and provide a more prominent solution to a small problem. Check this out for irony. The disciples are hanging out with Jesus, eyewitnesses to astonishing power, faith, and action, and in many situations, they are given the same opportunity to execute change. Yet, all the while, they had a hard time performing the very same thing they were experiencing due to limited vision and little faith. Well, we, too, are sometimes in the presence of greatness or someone endowing us with knowledge or resources, and yet we can't execute what we are experiencing because we can't Hyper-See. We can't see an alternate solution due to a lack of faith and belief.

Your biggest problem with innovation and vision not becoming corporeal in your life might be because you can't Hyper-See. Is your vision limited to only producing what you can see right in front of you, what you were told to look at as the only route to success? Just like the disciples exhibited, we have far too long been living to walk by what we see and not by what we believe... *walk by faith, not by sight.* To effectively Hyper-See, one must be full of faith, hope, courage, and absolutely NO SELF-DOUBT.

Where is self-doubt birthed from? Why would individuals doubt their skills, talents, abilities, and gifts? It could be due to sorrowful or traumatic moments earlier in your life. Maybe a significant person from birth instilled in you that you weren't talented and wouldn't amount to anything. Perhaps you were never shown the support, love, and proper nurturing needed during early childhood. These are all factors, but the most concrete component as to why a person can't Hyper-See—and the most destructive force behind a person not fulfilling their purpose—is FEAR! Before jumping into the following major Key touching on fear, let me share a quick allegory with you:

There was an ambitious dreamer named Cliff who happened to be on an all-inclusive vacation getaway. While on vacation, Cliff met his tour guide, Willy B, who would give Cliff a tour of this super popular vacation site. Willy B showed off all the attractions and amenities, not withholding nothing this place had to offer.

Seeing that Cliff was a first-time guest, and Willy B ensured that Cliff would get firsthand experience as to why this destination was such a hotspot for visitors to vacation year-round. Willy B would wow Cliff, room by room, of all the vices that kept people checking in day and night, never wanting to leave, and even if they wanted to, they would find themselves unable to—due to always coming back!

There was the room of LUST that was always sold out. Next door was GREED, which was hard to access because everyone there was selfish and did not want to share in the fun by giving up their spot. Across the hall stood ADDICTIONS that kept fathers away from their kids and mothers on the streets. As the tour proceeded, Willy B showed off the BAD-HABITS boom-boom room, which held individuals captive to never elevating in life.

Cliff was in awe of how long the VIP line was to get into Club Lying. Everyone in line told him how great their lives were, but it was hard for him to believe, given how bad off they looked. Then there was the CONTROL room, which shared its space with the POWER room, and only the shrewdest men occupied it. Up the stairs on the left was the intense room of HATE, where fights and riots were breaking out every five minutes; right across the hall was PRIDE, a jam-packed room and, ironically, tiny for so many puffed-up individuals.

KEY I: VISIONARY or Dreamer?

Willy B then took Cliff to the grand-daddy room of them all. Willy B regarded this room as his favorite of all the attractions at the resort. Not only was it secluded, but it had around-the-clock security and generated record-breaking numbers of tourists.

Cliff walked into the room and noticed an object in an illuminated glass case with a small beam of light reflecting on it from above. Everyone there seemed so sad and distressed. *This was the most incredible room of all!* The tourists seemed hooked to it and had no intention or motivation to walk out. The expressions on their faces looked as though they had been there for a long time and desperately needed someone to rescue them. The vibe in the room was as if they had no clue how they even got there. Cliff had an overwhelming feeling of grief and deep compassion for all the hopeless people. In Cliff's mind, he concluded that this was no vacation attraction but a Hopeless resort.

With a look of confusion, Cliff turned to Willy B. and asked, "What's so great about this room? Everyone here seems depressed, discouraged, and just hopeless. This room doesn't seem so grand. The only thing noticeable is that object that looks like a door wedge in the glass case."

Willy B replied, "Oh no, Cliff. It's much greater than that. This is the most prized of all the rooms at the resort. What you're looking at is the easiest and most successful lure to get people to spend so much time with me here. That is not a door wedge. What you're staring at in the glass case is SELF-DOUBT."

Reader, pay attention; here is what we call revelation knowledge. Self-doubt has the image of a door wedge because Willy B doesn't need much room for self-doubt to enter a person's heart and mind to wreak havoc. The small beam of light penetrates because that's all that is required for self-doubt to crack through and erupt; just a small crack is needed to break a person's confidence, shatter their vision, and destroy their faith. The slight damage completely disrupts their belief system, perspective, and foundation. This will ultimately cause them to become trapped in fear and doubt.

Once self-doubt sets in, fear immobilizes the body, mind, heart, and soul, and that person will be damaged unless a change takes course. What makes matters worse is that once self-doubt has become the individual's new identity, this encourages participation in the other vices that run rampant in a place and state of hopelessness.

It is easy to perceive how a person will inevitably venture off to other addictions and why they would seek alternative outlets, no matter the cost, to replace the loss of robbed hope. But, sadly, above all, the individual will become so defeated that weeds of doubt will disrupt the vision God planted in them, and they will succumb to remaining nothing but a barren producing dreamer.

The moment you allow self-doubt to become your master, your self-discipline will take a hit, you won't aspire to be great, you'll give up on yourself and your family, and you will finally become the ultimate quitter. Vision and Vertical Living are no longer within sight. Without a foundation to build on, your ground will be shaky and crumble when the test of time comes. If not dealt with appropriately, these new realities produced by self-doubt will eventually lead to some or all the other vices that will keep you from riding the wave of greatness and cause you to drown in the abyss of total failure. Ultimately, you'll give up.

Those who allow self-doubt to creep in invite addiction, depression, anxiety, and a defeated mindset to set in. Say this with me out loud, with total confidence and total conviction:

> *NO MORE SELF-DOUBT,*
> *NO MORE SELF-DOUBT,*
> *NO MORE SELF-SOUBT!*

This leads me to my third and final weapon needed to create the force that will enable you to travel from trials to triumph. This weapon

KEY I: VISIONARY or Dreamer?

will empower you to no longer be a dreamer but a VISIONARY, granting you access to VERTICAL LIVING!

Make Fear Your Tailwind

How much fear have you allowed to impact your life? Are you okay with dealing with that fear? Or are you ready to start overcoming that fear?

What does "making fear your tailwind" mean to you? Why should we transform our modus operandi into making fear our tailwind?

While watching an episode of Complex Blueprint on YouTube, I came across an episode interviewing one of the greatest musical visionaries of all time, Jimmy Iovine. Mr. Iovine was asked, *"What has been a major key to your success?"*

Jimmy paused and replied, "When I made fear my tailwind."

My jaw dropped; of all the answers this iconic, innovative visionary could have mustered up to say, that was one I wouldn't have counted on with a number line! But instead, the visual I inferred from this powerful statement was that of a vast ship.

In life, we often operate like a ship; we're on a destined course, and our overall success depends on what we allow to power us—getting us to the destination of whatever we deem valid and vital. Jimmy Iovine mastered the art of using pressure and fear to his advantage, never allowing it to put him at a disadvantage.

You can think of fear as a cloudy film that sticks to the lens of your vision; with enough of it built up, fear can blind you of your most tremendous potential, rob you of your greatest profit, and destroy any possibility of your ship getting you to the Promised Land. Speaking of the Promised Land, the children of Israel allowed fear to keep them wandering in a desert for 40 years when it should have only been a four-day journey (Exodus 3:18).

Because the children of Israel allowed fear to steer their ship, a generation never came close to encountering the Promised Land. I'm unsure if you know the story, but they were eyewitnesses to God's splendor, might, and power. Yet, even with God proving Himself mighty, they still allowed fear to debilitate their vision. Once enough fear sets in, doubt will become the new reasoning ... and when those two are playing on the same team, you lose trust in everything—even the truth.

Dreamers operate in all these categories because they have no vision, and their idea is non-apparent. After all, fear is the majority rule of their life. Dreamers doubt themselves because fear has prohibited them from exploring the greatness and vision inside of them. These types possess a vast gift but never unwrap it to see what it can produce; fear has prevented them from even noticing the package. For example, people who can sing their hearts out never audition for opportunities, which is why those who have an evident ability to lead are always following, and those who are tech-savvy only use gadgets but never create them.

BLAME FEAR FOR THAT.

> *When it comes to fear, the difference between someone who lives by fear and me is this: I never surrender to fear, and they are never in control of how they operate in fear!* —Wavie Iso Lee

Emotions play a massive role in how powerful fear flexes its muscles. Unfortunately, most individuals are too emotionally invested. Certain decisions, challenges, and opportunities are ruled more by emotion than logic. Being too emotionally invested can lead you to *react* with no sense, whereas, with reason, you can *respond* with wisdom. I've been a prisoner of my own emotional decisions many times, which has cost me dearly.

We must be cautious in what we allow to power and steer our visionary ship. When I heard Jimmy say, "Make fear your tailwind," I knew I had allowed fear to lead my ship for much of my life instead of fear being what propelled my ship. Jimmy said, "*The person who can harness fear and make it work for them as opposed to against them has the greatest advantage over his/her competition of those who can't harness fear.*"

Let's unpack this ship analogy bit by bit.

The crew on our ship consists of our gifts, talents, and visions—all of which work harmoniously as a unit, taking us to our greatness and ultimate destination of vertical living. Our opportunities, resources, and extensive networks would be our living quarters. The ship's anchor keeps us grounded when havoc erupts so that we can experience, endure, and overcome the storms of life—all while never veering off course.

When fear is steering our ship, two things occur:

1. Fear is causing you to make unwise decisions that keep you dreaming (going off course).
2. Fear prevents you from embarking on new endeavors and betting on yourself.

Confidence is used unconsciously and effortlessly when unintentionally speaking self-doubting affirmations over your life. In contrast, if we said, "I can, I will, I must," we would see a drastic spike in productivity, completion, and consistency in the areas of success we put our minds to.

What does a person who has made fear their tailwind look like?

It's the individual who writes a book and becomes an author, forever leaving a legacy. The kid who dropped out of college because he wouldn't allow fear to stop him from ensuring every person, place, and business had a PC using his software (Bill Gates). The person who uses fear to empower their life looks like the young lady who said, "I won't let opposition or fear stop me from sitting on the bench of the U.S. Supreme Court." The individual who has made fear their tailwind is the person who knows they'll fail but won't quit.

The person who makes fear work for them is that one inner-city kid who made up his mind, saying, "I won't allow my environment, my poverty, or my single-family household to make me sell dope, but instead, I'll go to M.I.T. and bring technological change to my neighborhood and sell hope."

This is YOU. This is ME.

This is US!

The person who has made fear their tailwind has learned to reprogram their mind and has begun to Hyper-See. They have started to see their vision vividly, in ultra 4K clarity, and realized that fear has prevented them from being able to Hyper-See.

Fear is a choice, not a condition. Your condition becomes the picture you've allowed fear to paint. Once fear has become fully birthed, you'll live and experience that reality. Many people kill their vision due to the fear of what others may say or think about them; they become in bondage to another person's opinion, negative perception, or dislike about them and their vision. You may have let comfort in your fears to allow you to live your life horizontally and not vertically.

Millions of people fear losing the "comfort" of working 40 hours a week, thus becoming dreadfully conjoined to their jobs for a miserably long time. I say miserably because, day in and day out, they're limited in utilizing the gift and vision inside them. They only experience a moment of freedom during March when they either receive their income tax return or take advantage of the two-week vacation they worked 365 days to get. What a despairing exchange! They're not even partially satisfied with doing what they weren't entirely created and designed to do.

Some fear losing out on a comfortable relationship that's not progressing. Some fear change and have no interest in taking a leap of faith to better their life and situation because it requires more of them.

As author Jordan Raynor so eloquently put it in his marvelous book, *Called to Create*, "An infinitely creative God created us to reflect his love and character to the world. One way we do that is by continuing His creative work."

How can you do that without being able to work on your passion part-time so that it squeezes out your full-time job? You should never permit being unable to express your creative gift because of fear of bills, the fear of just making it, and the fear of paying off the mortgage for the house you knew you couldn't afford.

Listen, I'm not anti-job, but I am aggressively anti-dreamer. I fully endorse and promote creative, enterprising, and volitional vision. I sincerely intend to provide you with another side of this perspective to be open to. I believe that you should be creating and doing what you are passionate about and find joy in completing it. But, of course, with prayer, patience, and Godly wisdom, we can prevail through grooming seasons and be faithful at our jobs while overcoming life's challenges. This undoubtedly, at many times, will come from a job you're not fond of. Yes, you must work a job at multiple points in your life! Yes, you need a vehicle through a job to assist in getting you to your potential and divine destination! There's nothing wrong with pursuing a career in the form of a job so long as you find purpose in it and plan to use the job as a new sacrifice for freedom later. In my opinion, only exchanging time for money is a bad deal.

The job should be viewed as a resource rather than the primary source. The position is only ground to sow on for God's glory and a tool to get your ship to the Promised Land.

The paycheck, a couple of annual pay bumps, and weekly vacations throughout the year are only temporary fixes after 15-20 years of fear. Don't get me wrong, if you have found vision and purpose in your career choice at your job, then I salute you. But if you're only doing that job because you've allowed fear to hold you back from genuinely recognizing your vision, I strongly encourage you to keep reading this book.

> *"Dreamers thrive in fear, only moving laterally because moving vertically makes them afraid of heights."* —Wavie Iso Lee

Making fear your tailwind is a necessity for becoming a VISIONARY. You may ask yourself, "How can I make fear my tailwind?" I've given you the first two in this one key.

Regarding fear itself, here are seven tips on how to turn fear into favor:

1. First, prepare for a major detox of undoing every negative thought you've allowed to run rent-free in your mind and life.
2. Purge yourself of every bad habit that has been contrary to your success.
3. Retune how you build your confidence.
4. Refine how you go about keeping your confidence.
5. Repair any parts of your ship that you've allowed fear to damage.
6. Don't forget the small wins.
7. Do recall past victories and reflect on how those victories made you feel.

Negative thoughts include the words CAN'T and TRY. Substitute them for CAN and WILL. Revitalize your mind by reading, listening, and mastering SELF-DISCIPLINE. Begin to read books by successful, positive individuals. When cooking, cleaning, or working out, occasionally try to replace workout music with audiobooks by millionaires, heavy critical thinkers, and leaders in their respective fields of study and expertise. Even for myself, at some point, you'll need to bang your

KEY I: VISIONARY or Dreamer?

favorite track to get you through the rest of your workout. During active growth, the mind is in one of its highest conscious states to receive and absorb the material you feed it.

You'll most certainly have to rid yourself of the company of pirates plundering your ship and keeping it from setting sail. How? The most common-sense way to do this is by starting to do everything fear doesn't allow.

Stop wasting free time and precious moments starving your mind; start capitalizing and cashing in by filling your mental psyche with life-changing information. For this to happen, you must renew your mind so that self-discipline becomes the new you, the new norm, and the new daily routine.

To master self-discipline, one must first learn to be in self-control as much as possible. In the Bible, the book of James says that a double-minded man is unstable in all his ways. What does this equate to? It is like a man who needs more self-discipline and self-control, who remains indecisive and can only make wise, practical decisions with it. Because of this instability and lack of self-discipline and self-control, this type of person is also subject to the harsh realities that life will undoubtedly throw their way.

The dreamer who is unstable is and will always be asleep. The dreamer, unstable in their ways, picks up and puts down, never remembering the purpose of what was picked up and why it was put down. The dreamer who is unstable is a vagabond—never being still but constantly bouncing around from career to career, job to job, relationship to relationship, and a bad idea to an even worse idea.

The overall goal of making fear your tailwind is to attain, gain, and apply as much fruitful knowledge as possible within the 24 hours of each day God allows us to live. Fear has caused powerful nations, organizations, and corporations to crumble because they believed their dream was too big to fail. Fear has caused the grave to fill up with ideas, inventors, medical breakthroughs, and solutions to global problems because those in that grave never tapped into their vision.

By harnessing fear and making it your tailwind, you will possess what many had no idea existed. When you decide to let fear be the fuel to your vision tank, powering you through, and not just the engine alone, then you'll be UNSTOPPABLE.

These steps, this vertical mindset, and this new weapon will equip you to see your VISION, become your VISION, display your VISION, and live your VISION.

Public Service Announcement: STOP DREAMING!

To recap, a reprogrammed mind, the ability to Hyper-See, and making fear your tailwind are critical weapons in destroying the drastic effects of fear. These life-enhancing tools will enable you to transform fear into your propeller and not the rudder of your ship.

> **INFORMATION WITH APPLICATION IS TRANSFORMATION!**

KEY II:
Execute. Complete. Repeat.

> "Innovation is rewarded, but EXECUTION is worshipped."
> —Eric Thomas

I would be a multi-millionaire a few times over if I were paid $100,000 every time I planned or prematurely started a goal or task and did not come close to executing that plan.

There's a significant difference between EXECUTING and COMPLETING. I would suggest that completion is contingent upon the due diligence and discipline of execution. Before we dive in, let's take a quick look at the definition of both execution and completion:

Execution (v)—To carry out; accomplish: (2) to perform or do.

Completion (adj)—Having all parts or elements; lacking nothing; whole; entire; full: (2) Finished; ended; concluded: (3) Having all the required or customary characteristics, skill, or the like; consummate; perfect in-kind quality.

Execution is a strict and rigorous practice and habit that many do not possess, and this is for a variety of reasons. For some, it can be due to a destitute upbringing, socioeconomic barriers, or even a bad investment of time following bankrupt examples from unqualified leaders. Other reasons could be a lack of desire or will to achieve and a lack of opportunities, including resources.

Various factors can greatly influence an individual's life, beginning with the home upbringing. The home is the nest where the feeding, nourishing, and instructing occur and where amounts of improper or prosperous seeds of knowledge, know-how, and discernment are planted. Perhaps you grew up having never been exposed to witnessing what execution looks like or feeling the rewarding results of what execution affords.

Take a moment to reflect on your life and try to recount all the times you were excited about starting a life-changing project or setting a new way of living for yourself that produced zero results and damaged productivity.

How does this time of reflection make you feel?

When I faced this "monster" in reflection, I oddly felt thankful—learning from those lost moments the importance of capitalizing on the blessing of time. Time allows you to turn those zeroes into whatever number you want. Because of the gift of time, you've survived to this point by the grace of God. But, although thankful, you shouldn't be comfortable just surviving but instead thriving. The proof of this divine moment is that you're reading this book. At this very moment and season, you're becoming empowered to improve your life and enhance your ability to EXECUTE!

This also shows the importance of how much collectively we need each other. In my life, I've concluded that people—an intentional network—are the most valuable commodity. Without the right people and a strong supporting cast, execution can be limited or even non-existent. Yes, we love to be independent while pursuing our passionate ambition. Still, we must

KEY II: Execute. Complete. Repeat.

surround ourselves with like-minded and forward-thinking individuals who will aid us on our quest to vertical living. I'm not talking about encounters that are only transactional but real-life solid building relational foundations. If I'm not the first to tell you, I can assure you that as a visionary, you will never have to fish for like-minded individuals on the same wave as you. You must be open to this reality, and your mind must be sharp in discerning those who are a compliment to your vision and those who are a stumbling block. The mission is for each other, not just for self.

Because of the lessons I learned and my experience of—not what I've been through but what I've GROWN through—this book is now a resource for your overall development, transforming you into an EXECUTING VISIONARY!

> *"We all are an extension of an extensive network for each other."* —Wavie Iso Lee

Looking back, I recount one of my toxic habits of being excited about new endeavors and never seeing it through or going any further than a mere thought. It was clear as to why I could never execute or complete anything. If you can remember, I would like you to think back on the many times you told yourself that you would be committed to something or even someone, and it went away as quickly as it came to you.

Did anything materialize? How do you feel about those times? How many people, friends, and family did you let down? How many of them do you believe would've benefited from your vision or idea?

What about when you were stoked about a new idea, investment, or career change that never saw the light of day? Then, as those moments race to the forefront of your mind, ask yourself:

Where are the promises and rich results of those plans?

Are they hidden? Did they happen, but you didn't realize it? Maybe, maybe not. The point is that it's not over! Your plans are not buried. They're just planted ... and waiting for you to water them with execution.

Look around and take note of what successes those long-term ideas brought you. Did you find any success? Next, glance at your checking account to see how much money you've accrued from the investments of time and energy you diligently put forth. How many figures do you have?

Everyone is an innovator in some respect, meaning everyone can cook up an idea and invention for their life or that of others; the reality check is that *not everyone can execute them.*

Many individuals don't have what it takes to endure and grind it out, to execute and apply those disciplines needed to surpass every initial idea and innovation. Those who lack the vision to achieve cannot conjure up multiple innovative ideas; they can always think it but lack the hunger to execute, complete, and repeat it. They lack the appropriate vision and desire to carry out the very thing they sought to do.

I was very malnourished in vision and desire because I was a dreamer and lacked self-discipline. I might have wanted a vertical life but wasn't ready to put in the discipline or work needed to accomplish it!

I wasn't willing to give 120% but was content with only 75%. See, it was the 75% that kept me dreaming; the 75% mentality allowed me to stay within a box of mediocrity and comfortability.

You can always tell who a 75% effort-type person is. You sense the 75-percenters—those who don't execute—because their life never reflects that of a 120-percenter—a visionary. The difference between these types boils down to the ability to EXECUTE! Trusting in God and your ability is the only way to find any real sense of completeness.

In the bible, there is an example where The Lord gave a demonstration about lack of execution and its negative results of producing no fruit:

KEY II: Execute. Complete. Repeat.

> "So, every good tree bears good fruit, but the bad tree bears bad fruit. A good tree cannot produce bad fruit, nor can a bad tree produce good fruit." (Matthew 7:16-20 NASB)

With that firm and solid principle, as well as a concrete idea, I desire to make every effort to keep the importance of a vision and the execution of it in the forefront of my mind. I encourage you to do the same. Unless you're genuinely executing with results to confirm, you'll never be able to produce the result for yourself so that you can pass it on to others. Harvesting on what you have planted will be difficult because the ground you have sown on –which you believed you have worked toward—will produce nothing but weeds, thorns, and thistles. Eventually, your work (efforts, dedication, discipline, and character) will expose you. The fruit you produce will reveal if you're legit or a fraud.

So, at this point, ask yourself: are you a dreamer or a visionary? Are you executing or just exiting? Whichever you are will show up in your daily life. It will show up in the office. On the field. In your children's lives. When it counts the most, it will be on full display. It will eventually become apparent to the outside world through your flourishing or perishing and ability to bring in a harvest or barrenness.

Individuals can only COMPLETE a goal by first EXECUTING the plan.

> *"The percentage you sow is the percentage you'll yield."* —Wavie Iso Lee

Lastly, quickly reflect on those moments I asked you to reflect on earlier. Take a moment and, with transparency, ask yourself, *"Why was I unable to execute?"* I want you to speak with bold conviction to yourself, making this statement:

"I apologize for always thinking, believing, and creating it but never EXECUTING it. Today, I commit to EXECUTING. Today, I promise to

COMPLETE, and today I will REPEAT!"

> **BELIEVE IT. SEE IT. BECOME IT.**

I don't know about you, but I felt great relief and rejuvenation when I spoke those words. I hope you did, too.

Switching gears, I'll be honest with you and offer some insight from my personal experiences on why I believe you might lack the focus to execute. First, let me sympathize with you; it's not entirely your fault. But, even more, you've chosen to implement change in at least one area of your life by first reading this book.

I will share the wisdom, knowledge, and power that has allowed me to EXECUTE, COMPLETE, and REPEAT.

I've already mentioned how your upbringing and dozens of factors surrounding your childhood might have excluded you from inheriting the discipline needed to execute. As you've increasingly become more aware of this, make it a point to no longer allow that to stop you from breaking the sound barrier for your life.

The beauty in birth is that we're first fully alive, living, and breathing. We have no choice but to grow and wise up, becoming responsible and accountable for the choices we decide on in life. It doesn't matter if your past disadvantages caused you to fail in your execution; at this very moment, you are gradually inching closer to vertical living, and those past choices and shortcomings are no longer a stumbling block for your life. These life choices—sometimes good and often harmful—are designed to teach us many things if we allow and learn from them. If that is the case, we will benefit from those lessons by gaining insight from those life experiences. "

> *There are only wins and lessons, no losses unless you quit."* —Wavie Iso Lee

KEY II: Execute. Complete. Repeat.

If you never learn that touching something hot burns, you'll never be aware of when you're placing yourself in HOT situations. Unfortunately, many dreamers never learn from the experiences that burn them. Many times in my own life, I find this to be true because of pride. Remember, in our allegory with Cliff, pride was an attraction many gravitated toward, all while never recognizing their errors. When pride interferes or gets in the way of life learning lessons, we go astray, seeking out alternate routes and shortcuts to touch what is hot—becoming numb to the fact that it burns or simply hoping it won't burn more the next time. As stated in a previous example, this behavior would be likened to insanity, constantly doing the same thing repeatedly, hoping for not just a different but favorable result. There's a safe bet you're behaving foolishly when this climax is reached. The generalization is that most will continue in life only looking for faster routes to burn themselves slower, hotter, and more ignorantly.

Listen to me, please! From a person who has had firsthand accounts of painful experiences by way of consequences, learn from them! Allow those experiences to be learned lessons so you don't repeat them. I want you to repeat execution, not error.

Another step that will lead you to increased and efficient execution is capitalizing *on life experiences.*

> **"Never let your old life define you,**
> **but always allow your past experiences to refine you."**

It can be advantageous when reflecting on some of the wins gained from life's lessons, even if some of those hard lessons were self-inflicted due to poor performance. What do I mean? Take those unsuccessful results you experienced due to poor discipline, not appropriately loving yourself, and committing to make unwise decisions. Allow those experiences to empower your future. Do your best to familiarize yourself with what negatively allowed you to be under the hump, and then recall what it was that got you over the hump.

I remember one night when I was homeless in the church basement of Overcomers in Christ Ministries... I was lying on a sofa that was too small because my legs were hanging off the end; I began to ponder on my past decision-making moments and asked myself, "How did I end up here? How did I, with all my potential, find myself sleeping in a church basement? What was it that I committed to that was so bad it resulted in me bathing in public restrooms?"

After a severe reflection, the answers came pouring in. I heard them loud and clear:

Can you recall how wasteful you've been over your many resources? What about how careless you were with your credit? Do you remember the many jobs you couldn't commit to for over three months? What about the times you never thought about the future of your children when you were living life solely for yourself as I was? How about the multiple relationships you never took the time to heal from properly?

Did you forget how you squandered lump sums of cash? How about the time you enrolled in college, taking loans you didn't need so that you could create more debt for yourself by blowing refund checks? This was me looking in the mirror. This was my defining moment of accountability. I would reflect this type of person consistently. So, my friend, let me share this truth with you. The consequences of your decisions are like a collection agency; you don't know when, but they will show up one day ready to collect on those moments of recklessness. It's all fun and games until the consequences want to play.

Now, where was I? Oh yeah, the sofa—at times, my mind can wander into these various rifts—those few moments were so intense I felt like I had died! It almost felt like there would be no recovery from my mistakes, and I would never be liberated from my self-inflicted prison. Although I was recounting all those difficult moments, the worst part

KEY II: Execute. Complete. Repeat.

was that it wasn't one of those single moments that led to my being homeless. *I created the very situation I was in due to an impoverished mentality.* I realized that I was committed to executing in areas of foolishness and repeating the same errors only in different situations. Whew! Those were some scary, dark moments of my life.

As in all things, there's always a glimmer of light at the end of a dark tunnel. There's always light in the tunnel as there is at the end of the tunnel. No matter how much you have made life difficult for yourself, there's always a mustard-seed-size of faith and hope that is strong enough to transform and turn your life around for the better completely.

> *"God doesn't cause the storms; He calms the storms."*
> —Senior Pastor, Pat Murray

It was at the very moment I began to capitalize on my life experiences. I committed myself to never return to that ditch of despair and agony. That ditch was full of poor choices, habits, and poor execution. Instead, my bad decisions prompted me to use an even bigger shovel of execution to dig myself out.

Life experiences, coupled with a humble heart, does *seven* things:

1. Teaches you to appreciate how sufficient God's grace is.
2. Endows you with a new elevated level of perception.
3. It opens you up to areas that need a good cleansing.
4. Guide you on a more purposeful path to vertical living.
5. Affords access to more significant advantages in your life's pursuit.
6. Gives you a higher appreciation for life.
7. Allow gratitude to rule your perspective.

Those seven statements are desires I want for you, including myself. God's grace covered me through all my reckless living and gave me a new appreciation for life and people. We must learn to appreciate what we have before we desire more. Appreciation, gratitude, and contentment are overlooked. These are simple and invaluable blessings to possess. There's not much I would deem more vital for you to possess in your personal and professional development arsenal. That was a groundbreaking and profound moment when I discovered the importance of those virtues, and additionally, it increased my desire never to be broke and mediocre again.

Gratitude and thankfulness allow you to rewrite mistakes and right the wrongs you have made so that you begin to execute and live out your purpose to its fullest potential.

If you recall, at the beginning of the book, I stated the importance of reading and how it would strengthen your personal and professional core for vertical living in addition to a life-giving conviction for your overall life. If applied, the keys from this book will teach you how to become a visionary, live vertically, and be a true reflection of greatness. This book will also plant seeds for being a more fruitful person, a better citizen, a dependable friend, an improved neighbor, etc.

It doesn't take extensive training, long hours studying new material, or labor to begin to execute. Sometimes, it just takes humility, gratitude, desire, and relentless willpower to change how you think and live. Overall, this isn't just for you to have for yourself but to share with others—passing along the wisdom you've gained to create a generation of visionaries.

I've realized that the greatest joy I get from doing what I do as a business owner, brand consultant, author, music artist, content creator, entrepreneur, and philanthropist is that I can use my gifts, skills, and resources to serve others. I can attest that what is most fulfilling for me is having a growing interest in the success of others more than myself.

KEY II: Execute. Complete. Repeat.

What is your definition of absolute happiness?

Happiness is the ultimate joy you feel while living toward your purpose. What would be the one thing you would do passionately that doesn't require an alarm clock, a paycheck, or advancement? Whatever that is, it is where your true joy and feeling of real purpose are made alive. And even if those things never come to pass how you want them to, you will still have complete joy because you are content with what you have and not what you want.

There is no real value in what you do if you're not impacting others to succeed just as well and, if not better, than yourself. This is what believers and followers of the teachings of Jesus would deem as having the mind of Christ.

> *You must have the same attitude that Christ Jesus had. Though He was God, He did not think of equality with God as something to cling to.*
>
> *Instead, He gave up his divine privileges; He took the humble position of an enslaved person and was born human.*
>
> *When He appeared in human form, He humbled himself in obedience to God and died a criminal's death on a cross.*
>
> *Therefore, God elevated him to the place of highest honor. and gave him the name above all other names, that in the name of Jesus, every knee should bow, in heaven and on earth and under the earth, and every tongue declare that Jesus Christ is Lord, to the glory of God the Father. (Philippians 2:5-11 NASB)*

Personally, the real major change took place when I began to dedicate the teachings of Christ to my personal and professional life. Once you complete this book, your journey to becoming a visionary and living life vertically, in addition to properly executing your vision, will aid you in avoiding the paths to ruin and destruction.

At the beginning of the chapter, I spoke about the importance of being under the tutelage of a qualified leader so that you can witness what real execution looks like. My main example was in the person and teachings of Jesus Christ and the life He lived leading up to His triumphant moment on the cross. Then there's my granddad, who showed me the school of hard knocks as an example in his daily life, and my dad, who always did what he could to make it happen. Moment by moment, day by day, step by step, story by story, both impressed upon me how to execute and be a true visionary.

While desperately seeking knowledge and wisdom, I learned how to execute appropriately and look for specific characteristics in great men that would add value and inner riches to my life. Of course, I'm not saying that a person should do precisely what I did and believe what I believe because results vary. Not everyone's situation is the same, but my life didn't change for the better until I developed a real, genuine relationship with Jesus Christ.

From my past to who I am now, I can only attribute that to God and family. I would be lying if I gave anything or anyone else in the world that credit. So, when I share my story, I tell people I'm a man of faith for you to witness my glory from God.

The path you take in whatever you do in life is according to your faith and your own belief. I share and have mine in Jesus Christ. If you disagree, my friend, it is okay because we're in this together. It's not a matter of whether I'm right and you're wrong or what I say is definitive, but that we share a common interest in obtaining vertical results is all that matters. A critical trait of a visionary is being mature and open to hearing another's viewpoint, belief, and rationality, even if it doesn't completely align with yours. This is by no means a license

KEY II: Execute. Complete. Repeat.

for the receiver to compromise but to observe the fruit of people and offer correction or advice when needed. Or just seeing another side of things from someone else's point of view. It promotes healthy conversations to explore and learn different alternatives from other people.

There are no biases here except if you decide to remain a dreamer. It's nothing personal; I'm just pro-vision.

Getting back on track, the second step allowing you to access the key to execute effectively is to engrain the triple Ds into your life: ***Die Daily to Deadly Habits.***

One critical deadly habit you must eliminate from your routine is PROCRASTINATION! This is undoubtedly a silent killer that robs you mentally, physically, and emotionally. A stone-cold vision killer is what I consider procrastination to be, as it has contributed to the deaths of hundreds of thousands of visions and plans.

Here's a bit of irony about procrastination being such a killer. It has never stepped foot in a courtroom to be tried and convicted of all the killing it commits. "How so?" you may ask.

Procrastination not only kills vision, but it also takes lives as well. Ponder how many people have died at the expense of an ignored doctor's order about their health … or how many people are intentionally negligent when it comes to proper diet and exercise due to procrastination.

The core of procrastination is that people believe every day is promised and have all the time in the world to make life happen. Such arrogance! This is the very trap and deceit of procrastination.

> *"One must learn to practice delayed gratification for future satisfaction."*

Yes, I'm sure you've heard some form of the effects of procrastination. I'm pretty sure I'm preaching to the choir, but I can assure you this: you've never heard procrastination discussed in the way I will share.

Have you taken inventory of procrastination in your own life?

Procrastination is such a silent and addictive habit. Procrastination is such a phenomenon that Malta, this tiny island in the central Mediterranean Sea, is considered the laziest country in the world, with a staggering 71% inactivity from its citizens.

Procrastination is symptomatic of a psychological derangement associated with numerous adverse and mental disorders such as depression, irrational behavior, low self-esteem, and anxiety. So, when I stated that procrastination kills, I was not just saying that for it to be taken lightly.

Procrastination is a severe disorder. It is so easy and comfortable to be lazy. Putting off essential things to sit around and watch TV or participate in something that adds no value to your life is enjoyable.

Many times in my life, I found it so much easier to be lazy than productive. So, which "pro" are you? Productive or Procrastinator?

Most individuals know what they should start doing rather than what they need to stop, but procrastinating derails the need to accomplish anything. This is also true when it comes to you executing your vision.

In my experience, I've noticed that the most highly "successful" procrastinators are the most advanced dreamers. They fail to comprehend that the deadly combination of dreaming and procrastinating simultaneously kills their present and future.

How have I come to this truth? I saw it in my daily action ... at least once a day, for sure. It mostly happened in the morning. I would come into direct contact with this individual in the mirror before washing my face. That individual was me; I was that dreamer and procrastinator.

Thankfully, eliminating procrastination is an achievable feat.

Procrastination is a curable disorder. You can overcome this deadly trait by creating a purposeful vision for your life, the life of your family, and the lives of those you want to impact significantly.

KEY II: Execute. Complete. Repeat.

It's all about finding meaning in your life by way of passion. This isn't the meaning you labor to obtain; this is the meaningfulness that is already embedded in your DNA.

When you locate purposeful meaning in yourself and identify yourself with your vision, you will most certainly tap into your passion—becoming driven. Applying what has been prescribed in this book can potentially serve as an antidote to eliminate procrastinating pathogens. It will provide you the most significant advantage over your obstacles and competition—which, remember, is first yourself. You must get out of your way before anyone else can get in your way. If not, then you're in for a long uphill battle.

As you awaken to this new sense of living, you will naturally—with discipline—apply these benefits and learn to capitalize on your life experiences. At this life-changing point of transformation, you will quickly realize procrastination has always been the catalyst for why you were never able to execute, to begin with.

Listen, my friend, I don't know about you, but I just had a *"light bulb"* moment ... I hope you did as well, as we are connecting the dots!

The third and final deadly habit you must die to daily is HESITATION. Hesitating to execute exposes seven things about a person:

1. They lack self-confidence.
2. They're unsure about the given.
3. They're easily persuaded to quit.
4. They cannot be decisive.
5. There's no single commitment to anything.
6. They find blame for their failure in anything and everybody else.
7. They are easily swayed to do the opposite of what they should and want to do.

Hesitation, for many, is the leading cause of unrealistic plans and opportunities that never develop. Hesitation is the reason so many ideas are never birthed into anything tangibly.

There are moments when you must be able to take quick, confident, and decisive action in your decision-making. All the great VISIONARY leaders, icons, and elite individuals have one thing in common: they don't HESITATE!

This class of individuals never hesitate in the moment and at the opportunity to break the sound barrier of life. In his excellent read, *Relentless*, Tim Grover writes about getting in the zone that propelled the greats such as Michael Jordan and Kobe Bryant to dominate at high levels.

Tim Grover is an amazing VISIONARY who has trained some of the greatest athletes and has advised some of the top executives in the business world with his no-excuse, no-nonsense, and always-stay-relentless approach to every area of your everyday life.

After reading Tim's book, I discovered that hesitation is a weakness and handicap that feeds off fear and being overly emotional regarding decision-making. Hesitation thrives in a person who is unable to accept the challenge of performing and making winning decisions under pressure.

Which athletes come to mind when you think of an elite individual who didn't suffer from hesitation? As mentioned above, Michael Jordan and Kobe Bryant are the fiercest competitors on and off the court. They approached and attacked every aspect of life from this killer instinct mindset. There wasn't a shot that neither one of these two felt they couldn't take and at the same time make. For MJ and Kobe, not taking the final shot with the game on the line was worse than missing the last shot.

When opposing players and even teammates would let fear grip their nerves, MJ & Kobe relished in that moment of uncertainty. Then, when the game was on the line, and the win would be decided by one possession, the whole arena—including their opponent—knew who

KEY II: Execute. Complete. Repeat.

was taking the final shot. Michael, Kobe, and Tiger Woods are masters at execution. They were great at never hesitating and consistently executing because they pushed themselves to levels ordinary people wouldn't dare attempt. There was a necessity to execute, and each had a drive matched with an intense vision that no one else could perceive or even dared try to see and live through.

What separates the greats from the good, the visionary from the dreamer, and the doer from the hearer? First, there is a specific type of planning that one must consider to be able to take the last shot and make the last shot.

Execution for Jordan, Bryant, and Woods started when the last day of the season ended and the very first day of summer break began. There were never any breaks or moments to let off the gas. They were already in the gym and teeing off on the green, putting in work right after winning a championship or getting eliminated from winning one. If these three greats considered hesitating, feared, or could not lock in on executing with intense focus, you had better believe their names wouldn't have even been mentioned in this book. They wouldn't be worth mentioning. There would be no trace of who they are.

Reflect on the quote I used at the beginning of the chapter. Well, it could be applied through the lens of sports, "Those who make shots are rewarded, but those who hit game-winning shots are worshipped!"

Those who execute WIN CHAMPIONSHIPS!

Do not allow hesitation to keep you from having your name engraved in the record books of life. Never let being hesitant keep you from striking gold in your pursuit of greatness. Hesitation wants to abort your legendary status. Reluctancy only leads to a life of would've, should've, and could've. Those who hesitate live with regret for what they never were able to accomplish.

When you hesitate to make impactful decisions, you cripple your destiny of becoming iconic. However, there are moments when you must consider with much thought what choices to make ... and only when and if it would negatively impact your vision, greatness, and likelihood of vertical living. This type of hesitation comes when wisdom has kicked in; with the proper knowledge, you'll be equipped to make a profitable decision when you cross that path.

I previously mentioned those seven characteristics of one who hesitates: Of the seven, I believe the 2nd (they're unsure about the given) can be the most demoralizing to an individual's vision and stake at vertical living. When you hesitate about what is evident, your vision is at risk and needs significant correction. You lack major assurance in your ability, skill, and belief required to soar above mediocrity.

Any time you're faced with a decision that reveals the most remarkable outcome and reward, yet you still hesitate, you lack confidence and have a broken belief system. This type of individual has become well acquainted with being comfortable with mediocrity. Your spirit is broken because you have allowed fear to steer your ship and not propel your ship.

Now, there are some cases where a person's talent and skill can elevate them quickly to successful places their confidence, morals, and work ethic can't handle. What good is having a million-dollar idea with a hundred-dollar work ethic and moral compass? Does your gift make room for a six-figure income, but your integrity is minimum wage? I would compare it to a person who wins a talent contest as a singer but doesn't have the desire to write lyrics, learn musical arrangement, or put in heavy studio time. In short, this person has no desire to add more value to their brand, talent, and life.

This type of hesitant individual loves singing and wants to attract all the glory that being a superstar singer can bring, but doesn't want to boss up and become more. To level up and become more, one must do what is no longer comfortable and commit to becoming a sponge—learning as much as possible and doing all the things that aren't comfy, cozy, and easy.

KEY II: Execute. Complete. Repeat.

Recall what I said about the dysfunctional relationship between a dreamer and a visionary. **THEY CAN'T CO-EXIST!**

The singer will only learn how to execute if he or she hesitates to decide and commit to becoming more than just someone with a talented voice. I'm conveying that hesitation can be shown in many forms—not just in what you should or shouldn't do now, but also in how and when you decide to become better than great.

Deciding and executing when to be **PHENOMENAL** means you're no longer hesitant.

> *"Good business leaders create the vision, articulate it, passionately own it, and relentlessly drive it to completion."* —Jack Welch

Complete and Repeat

Let's talk about it.

Toward the end of March 2016, I decided to create, record, and engineer my first studio EP titled "D.O.P.E: Disciple on Planet Earth." At this point in my life, I was a local, up-and-coming, independent Christian hip-hop artist. I realized that to reach the next level of my early career, I would need to become a student to understand music truly. I needed to study and learn more about what it takes to be a complete artist.

It would require more than just being able to write and record my music and lyrics; I would need to train my ear to listen to music and develop an ear for editing, mixing, and mastering my music. Reprogramming my mind on how to step outside the boundary and comfort level of myself would be a must for my life to match my vision— at least musically.

During my early stages, I was paying engineers to execute the post-work on my projects, and most times, I wasn't getting the sound I heard and sonically seen during the creation phase of the recording process. Especially what I initially heard in my head before recording. One exception was my good friend Desmond J from Cincinnati, an already-known artist and music engineer in the Christian hip-hop community in Dayton and Cincinnati.

His sound and style inspired me, and I desperately wanted to wear multiple hats as an independent artist, which, over time, becomes natural to you in that field. But you will quickly know that "I have to become more than just a prototype." This would be especially true in the music industry.

Being an indie artist means you must do everything yourself. Suppose you don't have the luxury of everything being made available to you, e.g., studio, producer, industry connections, big budget, marketing team, etc., as you grow, learn, and become better. In that case of being independent and staying consistent, you'll attract the right community of people who will become valuable, hands-on, and instrumental in your development and success. I knew that while having a small budget and for this project's overall success and completion, I would need to acquire an ear for not just music but for sound frequencies, Eq, compression, distortion, and accurate volume leveling—to name a few.

So, what did that mean for me? It told me I must seek knowledge that lazy-hearted and lazy-minded dreamers can't cope with. I was sold on improving, so I locked in on the task. I began recording the project, working on my craft, and spending endless hours on YouTube watching tutorials and how-to videos on how to mix and master my music. I spent countless hours after hours practicing, messing up, starting over, and doing it again. I spent day after day perfecting, failing, and taking notes on editing and increasing my workflow's efficiency, mixing, and mastering.

I was breaking sound barriers.

KEY II: Execute. Complete. Repeat.

I was learning how to EXECUTE, COMPLETE, and REPEAT.

I studied the best music engineers YouTube had to offer and even innovated on their practices, creating my style, sound, and approach from the techniques they were providing. During that time, I had broken myself into this new routine by reading a few books on finances, investing, and forming business entities; so, for me, it was never a burden to hit the library and read a couple of books on music theory, proper mixing techniques, and how to navigate the music industry properly.

When it was all said and done, I started the project in March with a target date of April for release.

Did that happen? Of course not! The project dropped a couple of months later, but I was satisfied with the results of the work I accomplished.

However, at the same time, I began to morph into one who knows how to execute during the entire process. I was executing what I set out to do: becoming more skilled in the post-work of audio production, and I was eliminating laziness, comfortability, and lack of self-discipline.

I never had a problem locking myself in the studio to record for hours; I could do that in my sleep. However, my issue was being able to attack and apply the knowledge needed to become better and attain that next level in my pursuit. I was completely sold on the idea that if I believed it, I could become it, and that very same thought goes for you as well.

Realizing I needed to learn something new, my lazy heart didn't embrace this new habit. However, after reprogramming my mind and conditioning myself to make it my routine, it became more accessible and enjoyable. Finally, after getting a small taste of the fruit of execution, I saw it through to completion … and the feeling of fulfillment led to a desire to repeat.

> *"When you recognize that you must EXECUTE or fail, that'll determine the high level of intensity you apply toward your desired success!* —Wavie Iso Lee

I began to love the feeling and fruit of executing and completing something I would only read about others doing. I became compulsive and obsessed with *perfecting my practice*. I knew I could never be perfect, but I realized that perfecting my practice would lead to a permanent performance over time. So, after recording all the vocals, I began to do the post-work. Surprisingly, the EP wasn't released on iTunes until October 11, 2016, five days before my birthday, which felt good.

After the release of my project, it felt as though I had tapped into my inner greatness, struck gold, and relished what it felt like to EXECUTE, COMPLETE, & REPEAT. For six months, I would watch those same YouTube videos, taking away something new each time. I was able to revise the individual tracks, re-level the volume, re-edit the effects, and re-mix and master six songs at least five days out of the week.

I did this until I knew I could truthfully walk away, saying, "I gave that project everything I had in me."

I use the example of my EP to illustrate and encourage you that we are often privileged with a challenging moment in life that creates conflicts and barriers within us, allowing us to become ICONIC. A famous status and iconic feeling will not always prove itself with glitz and glam or receive glorious recognition from the world. It's a sure fact you won't be awarded with a platinum plaque or a certificate of outstanding achievement. Your direct impact will not always be met with a considerable bank account, a mansion, or a Rolls Royce sitting in the driveway.

The iconic status is birthed within and only credited to its creator—YOU! Had I fallen victim to one of our deadly habits—one being *hesitation*, not buckling down, and learning a new skill that would add value to my career and life—I wouldn't be the visionary I'm increasingly becoming each day I'm blessed to experience. And I, indeed, wouldn't be dedicated to commitment and a daily desire to improve. I certainly would not have been able to complete this book to instill in you how to birth vision and live vertically.

KEY II: Execute. Complete. Repeat.

The most fascinating blessing from my EP was being able to witness and experience what I was made of; I truly evolved into a visionary who could EXECUTE. This accomplishment unveiled the secret to COMPLETION and taught me how to REPEAT consistently. I learned how to become more prominent than my struggles, challenges, and adverse moments in life. I also realized that total dependence and trust in God would be my greatest asset during my journey.

When positioned in the heat of the battle of challenging moments to become not just great or even phenomenal but extraordinary, don't hesitate to take the opportunity; relish the moment and embrace the challenge.

Remember, my friend, you are your biggest competition because only you can stop yourself. Recalling the book's introduction, I stated there was only one problem prohibiting you from taking flight and breaking the sound barrier to becoming a VISIONARY. And that problem has and will always be YOU if you continually fail to convert information into application.

Repeat this out loud with me:

> *"I desire to execute, I'm destined to complete, and I'm determined to repeat!"* —Wavie Iso Lee

KEY III:
Place. Position. Perform.

> "Never become satisfied with 2nd place in anything in life. Placing 2nd doesn't make you a winner, only the first loser!"
> —Wavie Iso Lee

Regarding different success levels, some people with the greatest success stories attain those high levels of vertical living by being in the right place, at the right moment, and born at the right time.

For example, if LeBron James hadn't been born in 1984, would he still have been the number #1 pick of the 2003 NBA draft? What would have been the outcome of Warren Buffet's life had he been born in Brooklyn, NY, and not Omaha, Nebraska? If Steve Jobs attended MIT and not Reed College, would we still have the iPhone? All three of these greats have this one thing in common: they seized the moment in the right place, space, and time. You can't argue or deny it!

This thought aligns with this chapter's key concept: *"Place. Position. Perform."* But there is another phrase I would like to use to shake things up a bit—to sum up those "what ifs" I mentioned ... and if I'm being honest, you're sometimes going to need "pure luck." Again, you can't argue or deny it!

Of course, hard work, dedication, commitment, persistence, and discipline contribute significantly to the success of those riding that elusive wave of high success. But the most overt component of those who reach that preeminent ladder of success was partly due to some *pure luck or, as many others would put it, their big break.* When you think about it, there's so much luck or good fortune involved that you can't at least consider it. LeBron James played four years of high school basketball plus every summer on the National AAU circuit. He remained injury-free leading up to being drafted by the Cleveland Cavilers. His dedication to his body and working on his game has led to him being the NBA's all-time scoring leader 20 years later. That's not to mention random freak accidents that could've happened and didn't. You can't rule out luck or just being extremely fortunate. Can you?

I've come to experience in my own life that pure luck can knock you completely out of contention for things you desire in life, no matter how hard you work for them. This is what I like to refer to as a type of vanity. I'm sure you can think of at least one person you know personally that has pursued plans and didn't even work one-third of their butt off to get it yet is reaping the benefits effortlessly.

One meaning of pure luck is like an individual correctly having all six numbers for the Powerball. Only one in millions hit the jackpot. Then there's another type of pure luck: to have perfectly *placed* yourself in the proper *position* to effectively *perform* at the *perfect* time, thus granting life-changing results.

There are occurrences where individuals have luckily won millions of dollars or stumbled upon great success, but it didn't last long for many reasons. Some individuals stopped putting in the work to maintain that level of success; others lost sight of their vision and became blind due to distractions. For others, their character couldn't handle the sudden rise of fame and fortune.

Here's the reality check I want you to cash quickly: hard work will not always be able to compete with and remain victorious over this type of pure luck. You must accept that and take the wins as they come.

KEY III: Place. Position. Perform.

With a grateful attitude and disposition, if you can't star in a blockbuster film as an actor but can help direct it, count that as a win. One perspective that I believe will keep you on the hunt for vertical living is accepting that everything will not always go as expected or hoped for all the time. There will come a point in your pursuit where the perspective of what you're striving for may never come to pass in totality. It would be worthwhile to press on to make life happen for you in the best and most fulfilling way possible. But as a concession, if you position yourself and take the wins as they come, you will experience positive results and a constantly fulfilled life.

As I previously stated, the pure luck I'm speaking of is not your typical definition. Pure luck revolves around the mentioned factors: the right place, moment, and time.

Here's an example of what I mean by how pure luck, as it pertains to this key's title, can supersede hard work. Let's say two equally talented actors are auditioning for the same leading role in a blockbuster film.

Actor A puts in 20 hours a week perfecting their craft, showing up early, memorizing their lines, and was given an audition time of 9:00 a.m.

Actor B, who puts in 7 hours a week honing their acting skills, showed up on time, was prepared, and had an audition time of 9:30 a.m.

During the auditions, Actor A crushed the performance in front of the casting team, who also stated they were terrific. Actor B also showed up and dominated their audition in front of the same staff, except for the lead casting director, who sat in on their audition.

Who do you think got the role and why?

You possibly could've chosen Actor A … but why? Could it have been because they worked extra hard and did everything right?

Did you select Actor B? What would've granted them victory over who seemed to be the obvious choice in Actor A?

Could it have been due to Actor B's position—being able to *perform* in front of the lead casting director at the right *time*? I'm pretty sure the amount of time both talents put into preparing may have also caught your attention. But as you can see, based on the outcome, the amount of work put in didn't matter during the audition, especially when they both showed up to make a profound impression.

So many variables exist to consider why Actor A came in second place. What Actor A couldn't plan for, or outwork was the pure luck that would be on Actor B's side. And that luck collided and crashed Actor A's hopes of landing the role.

Those variables all point to the pure luck factor of the right place, moment, and time to position and perform. But that's not where it stopped.

I don't want to spend much time going through all the different scenarios. Yet, to provide you with an example, we could consider that, solely based on the time slot Actor B was given and ultimately selected, that was a **suitable time** for that individual to get the role. We could also assimilate that Actor B being able to perform in front of the lead casting director was at the *right time.*

Lastly, whatever came about for Actor B to get the 9:30 a.m. audition instead of the 9:00 a.m. audition was due to her being in the **right place** when initially scheduling the audition. I call this 50/50 diluted pure luck: fifty percent hard work and fifty percent pure luck. That makes sense. Yes. No. Maybe not.

So, now you're asking, "How can I have favorable odds when competing against pure luck?"

I suggest you become like the opposition. For this example, let's say that pure luck is your enemy, and I'm telling you to use your enemy's tactics as your weapon. I just gave you the key ingredients of pure luck, so why not use those same ingredients in your own life to pursue success?

To compete with pure luck and your competition, you must *Place* yourself in every favorable environment as much as possible, then firmly *Position* yourself in every favorable situation. Finally, with every promising opportunity, you must *Perform* like your life depends on it.

KEY III: Place. Position. Perform.

> *"Commit to SUCCESS & play to WIN."* —T. Harv

Using this formula to attack and conquer your life's pursuits will render you the desired results with at least a 25% advantage over the competition. It will take a relentless work ethic and an ability to truly get in the zone, all while responding to pressure by applying pressure.

It will surely pay off to incorporate this mentality with precision in addition to what you've learned from reading this book. If you apply these principles by creating a daily routine, you can easily make LIFE HAPPEN FOR YOU AND NOT ALLOW LIFE TO HAPPEN TO YOU.

At this point, you must become calculated and strategic in your skillset, talent, and opportunities—including what options you should consider. Then, mark your lane as your territory and dominate it viciously. There is no time to switch vision lanes; when you deviate from your lane of purpose, you give your opponent the upper hand, increasing the odds of pure luck working *against* you and in your opponent's favor.

Remember that hard work will not always be enough to stand victorious over pure luck ... but using the same principles described gives you a fighting chance to create and reach your destiny, ultimately becoming a VISIONARY and no longer a dreamer.

Once you have decided that your vision of success greatly depends on how you place and position yourself and, importantly, *perform*, I guarantee you that the averages of your successful results will significantly increase.

The performance department is the most important of the three; placement and positioning amount to nothing if you don't execute and perform. Actor B was in the right moment and time but would've remained jobless had they not PERFORMED.

> *"When given a seat at the table of success, if you don't perform, you don't eat."* —Wavie Iso Lee

Now, I hope the insight provided into some disciplines needed to hit monumental levels of vertical living was helpful to you. Being able to perform is contingent on how much work you put into owning your craft, staying true to your vision, and conditioning yourself to improve. Putting extra time off the clock will position you and better prepare you to perform at the right place and time. Over time, you will create higher success rates in everything you do, no matter the results.

Applying these principles practically to your life will ensure you improve in the other areas you may lack. This will create a domino effect, spilling over into those neglected areas of your life that need improvements. For example, you'll become a better spouse and an improved listener if you're a sub-par spouse in that category. If you have not been the best parent, you'll set better examples for your child(ren) in healthy and positive ways. There will be an emphasis on not wasting time, and your productive approach will become more intentional, purposeful, reliable, etc. Everything about you will become sharper when you apply the keys and applications from this book.

Placement, positioning, and performance greatly impact whether you're placing first or not placing at all—coming in second place means that you were first to lose-. "First place only" must be a new attitude and mentality ... even if you don't always come in first. It doesn't matter if your mental sharpness and preparation are always set on finishing first. All that matters is having a FIRST PLACE WINNING MINDSET!

There is nothing arrogant or egotistic about constantly pushing yourself to finish first so long as it doesn't compromise, diminish, or blemish your character and integrity. That type of mindset will challenge you to become legendary. When those three components are compulsively applied to your life, you'll stay ready so that you'll always be ready.

Learning how to position yourself means you don't waste time or opportunities. It means you capitalize on every place you've set yourself to be.

KEY III: Place. Position. Perform.

Those who aren't disciplined enough to stay in their lane will take themselves out of position and contention by veering off into lanes unsuitable for their destination. This is like busting your butt only to find that you've been hustling backward, believing that it's getting you closer to the front of the line of your success. Knowing where to place yourself is of vital importance. Knowing how to position yourself even when outmatched will come in handy. MJ & Kobe were still dominant in the later parts of their careers. Why? One aspect is that as they became more seasoned and understood the game's dynamics, the more they processed game situations, the more the game slowed down, enhancing their basketball IQ, which rendered it to their advantage. They knew where and how to pick their spots and were game possessions ahead to be in the proper *position at the right time to strike and execute, thus allowing a commanding performance.*

If you have the vision to be one of the most outstanding engineers of our time, why would you consider getting your degree from an institution that isn't engineered-focused? The point emphasized is that you need to be placed at a university that is concentrated on engineering, surrounded by only engineers, and only doing what engineers do, at least for the most part.

How you place yourself in preparation determines how and in what place you finish.

Placing yourself in favorable situations will reward you with a profitable outcome, a very high percentage of your attempts. Putting yourself in the proper position will consistently bring amazing results and a positive experience. Often, we experience growth moments that appear negative only so that we can truly learn from them… this is *capitalizing on life experiences.* Placing yourself in a favorable position but at the wrong time can be detrimental to the outcome of your vision and the level of vertical living you are pursuing.

For example, unhealthy relationships can lead to toxic positioning, leaving you out of place in your positioning. Surrounding yourself with an unproductive circle of friends can lead to stationary and stagnant placement. Lastly, poor habits combined with a scanty work ethic will always result in a lackluster performance, a broken mindset, and, even worse, a struggling bank account.

To recap, remember to be mindful of these three things and how they can work harmoniously: ***placement, positioning, and performance.*** Keep in mind that luck works just as hard as you!

Confirm this by saying to yourself out loud:

> *"I will place myself in the best situations;*
> *I will position myself for greatness;*
> *I will give my best performance in every opportunity!"*

KEY IV:
Master the Step-Back Effect

> "I hated every minute of training, but I said,
> 'Don't quit. Suffer now and live
> the rest of your life as a champion.'"
> —Muhammad Ali

What is the step-back effect? I would suggest the step-back effect is the most constructive and robust form of life training that will create champions. The step-back effect has many forms—various components that will either break a person down to the point of giving up or build a person up to finish triumphantly.

I came to realize, at a significant point of growing pains in my life, that I was going forward so fast in the pursuit of my vision that I was unintentionally disqualifying myself from proper training along the course. This training, in the form of adversity, would surprisingly spring up during great strides toward many of my goals, and it would start when I wasn't prepared.

Although I'm using the term adversity, I'm referring to those life experiences where you either must take a step back or God, in all His sovereignty, allows a season in your life where a sequence of events occurs that prepares you to step up. Unfortunately, it often feels like you're taking significant, heartbreaking steps backward from all your progress.

YOU'RE NOT HIGH ENOUGH

When I signed my placement deal with Crucial Music, I prematurely relocated to Los Angeles to chase a dream. To my surprise, I experienced a harsh reality leading to a severe crash and burn due to forgoing proper training. What I perceived to be something more than it was because I made it up in my mind that things would miraculously work for me and success would find me. I was gravely mistaken. That, my friend, is dreaming at it is finest. This is also an example of where presumptuous faith can land you in some challenging situations. What I perceived to be a highlighted moment in my life became a depressing and struggling nightmare. This nightmare became such a reality that I was forced to move back to Dayton, which at many moments was an environmentally depressing trigger, or I could have opted for sharing a box with people experiencing homelessness on Skid Row. Had I, at that time, been able to have already mastered the step-back effect, things would've turned out completely different.

All was not bad during my time in LA, and reaching new levels of success showed itself in a small glimpse of promise and success. There was a decent amount of highlight moments; I still had broken new ground in my music career, was able to perform on the biggest open-mic stage in the world at DPL (Da Poetry Lounge), and got a taste of what would become the birthing of my acting career—making a small appearance on the new TV show then called "Grown-ish."

It was life-changing—walking around Disney Studios in Burbank, CA, and getting a firsthand experience of Hollywood production was awe-inspiring. But even those glorious moments didn't take away what it took to reach that beginning amount of success. It indeed came at a cost.

I'm sure you've heard the phrase, "Nothing in life is free." Well, it's true. However, my quick and growing window of success initially came at the price of being away from my kids and family for over five months. During those strenuous moments, I had to exercise my ability to endure, be content with having little, and respond positively to

KEY IV: Master the Step-Back Effect

negative situations—all while patiently waiting on what I believed God enabled me to envision the success that awaited me. Lastly, I had to stay *consistently persistent*.

There were moments when I didn't know where I would lay my head the next night and many times, I feared having all my luggage and bags traveling with me while living on the streets of Vine and Hollywood Blvd. So many people's vision, passion, and pursuit become broken and hopeless in this part of LA, leading to homelessness. I feared this happening to me, but at the same time, every time, I took notice, and that kept me awake enough not to fall asleep on the mission. I questioned if what I was doing and going through was worth the trouble and risk. Even in my courageous and vigorous faith in the Lord, I often didn't see the light at the end of the tunnel.

Now, before I continue with my "started from the bottom" story and offer the key to how to master the step-back effect, I want to illustrate how advantageous a weapon this can be for you from now on in life. Suppose you're a fan of the game of basketball and the game's evolution of offensive moves. If you're not, I'll shed some light on this concept. In basketball, we have come to enjoy (and be amazed by) pioneers who have patented many dope, creative, and unstoppable moves to enrich the game and make it more entertaining.

To throw out a few names and moves, when you think of Kareem Abdul-Jabbar, you get the skyhook; Magic Johnson, the no-look pass; Michael Jordan, the infamous fade-away jump shot; Allen Iverson, his culture-changing crossover; most slept-on legend God Shammgod and his Shamgod Rollout move; and lastly, James Harden, Kevin Durant, and Steph Curry to name a few have mastered the signature move, which is called the STEP-BACK!

The step-back is a move one must possess to be an elite scorer in basketball ... and off the court to ball in life. When examining the move, the offensive player creates sporadic and spontaneous space, oddly going *away* from the basket. Once the offensive player's momentum has shifted and the defense is helpless, the offensive player has many options. Those options include a jump shot, or the offensive player could perform a move and blow by the defender if the defense is anticipating a jump shot.

The step-back is also universal; while moving laterally toward the basket, the offensive player can stop on the dime to step back for a three-point shot, thus avoiding the help defense in addition to gaining an advantage over the defender in a one-on-one situation, creating enough space for an uncontested jump-shot or a pass—leading to a high percentage bucket. In my efforts to explain, I hope that made 100% sense to you. If you don't play or watch basketball, I suggest searching it on YouTube. James Harden, in my opinion, more than any player mentioned, has worked on this move so much that he owns it; the step-back has become his bread and butter on the court and creates all types of havoc for a coach's defensive scheme. This move has contributed to Harden's luxurious contract, endorsement deals, MVP, and scoring records. The step-back has many perks to it if done and used appropriately.

Why would such a move be so effective and dynamic? How could James Harden gain an advantage by executing a dribble move that takes him *away* from the basket when the goal is to drive *toward* the basket or create non-contested jump shots? The answer is quite simple. James Harden has mastered not just the step-back but the effects of the step-back. And so can you in your life and your pursuit of Vertical-Living.

When you master anything, you are considered an expert in that field and are blessed to create favorable situations for yourself. Mastering the step-back effect in your life will allow you to implement positive and successful results for yourself and consistently and emphatically impact those around you. Not to mention the rewards of taking advantage of mastering the step-back as it can make all the difference in your bank account, career, status, and completion of endeavors.

KEY IV: Master the Step-Back Effect

Mastering the step-back effect also depends on your ability to capitalize effectively on your life experiences. Every experience in life, good or not so good, comes in the form of vigorous training that will create a more dynamic champion or an easily conquered quitter. For example, there was a moment in my journey when I made impressive strides in Hollywood.

Then, In the blink of an eye, I found myself back in the cold rigidness of Dayton, Ohio. I'll be honest: environmental depression set in for a couple of days because I was allowing what I presumed to be a setback to become my bully and reality. I was disappointed, leaving behind what I believed I had worked hard to accomplish. All that effort, dedication, and commitment, only to return to a place with nothing to offer me. Once I was able to tactically tap into what God wanted me to realize and analyze at the time, I began to grasp that this wasn't a setback but a moment to *step* back so that my springing forward would be even greater than before.

James Harden has mastered a move that allows him to create space from his defender and allow multiple options and opportunities for his teammates by simply and effectively stepping back. These things will undoubtedly happen when you realize the power of the step-back effect and master it appropriately.

Think about a time when you were moving forward in pursuing a goal, career change, relationship, etc., and something along the way caused a halt, which placed you further back than when you initially started. As you read this chapter, you might be in the eye of that storm right now. Let's apply the step-back effect to this scenario! As a quick side note, there are moments when we can become confused by lateral moves, mistaking them as vertical moments. If you're a manager in training at McDonald's and take a team lead position at Burger King because they will pay you $1 more an hour, that's not a promotion or a vertical move. That's not even a step-back moment; it's a horizontal move that looks like progression.

That would be a small example from working a job point of view, but this can also be viewed from a personal lens so that you get the point when you make confident decisions in life or take a particular risk, the results won't be horizontal which creates no additional opportunities or space to allow vertical living.

We know that the step-back effect creates space. So, when applied to your situation, it allows you to have a moment that I like to call (RTC) **real-time clarity**. This space lets you consider things that will be done differently when you get back on track with your vision and purpose. Taking a step back from a situation gives you a moment of much-needed solitude so that your *next* move will be your *best* move.

Things were happening at such a fast pace while I was living in LA. It was challenging to think straight. My mind was moving so fast that my thoughts couldn't catch up to what I was physically and mentally experiencing. Taking a step back grants you time to avoid making mistakes you don't realize you're potentially making. This is a technique and ideology that will genuinely benefit you, for sure.

The step-back is a basketball move, creating more options for the offense than the defense would like to allow. There are barriers in life that are set up just like a team's defense in that multiple oppositions are trying to impede your progress to scoring life buckets. When you make the most out of a situation where you must step back, this is the perfect time to draw on that experience and search out options on whether to pass or shoot.

Sometimes, we want to shoot when we really should be passing; sometimes, we pass on life because we didn't have the confidence to take the shot. This will often be true even when it comes to opportunities. This undoubtedly happens because we're too focused on what happens if I don't make the shot before even taking the shot. This also could translate to other moments of life where we attempt to control the situation or outcome we have no power over. Mastering the

KEY IV: Master the Step-Back Effect

step-back effect is like "going back to the future" to better your current. That sounds odd and yet genius at the same time. How do you go back to where you've never been? I'm just thinking out loud on paper.

My friend, this primary key is to be seen as a "ten commandments" for your life, vision, and career: Please find time during your morning or daily routine to recite these aloud at least once daily. You will begin to experience significant changes and results leading to Vertical-Living.

I COMMAND …

1. Restored confidence in all my abilities!
2. To know that having to take a step back doesn't mean the vision won't move forward!
3. To know and believe that there are only WINS and LESSONS!
4. My mind and heart are blessed with wisdom in making prosperous and profitable decisions!
5. The broken pieces in my life shall be corrected and fixed, shaping and forming a better version of me!
6. I shall remove all self-doubt!
7. I will make fear my tailwind!
8. I will experience an increase in vision & clarity!
9. I will lean on God to be my GPS instead of following my sense of direction!
10. I will EXECUTE for the rest of my productive life!

KEY V:
Be Driven, Not Motivated

What does it mean to be motivated?

How much motivation do you need to break the sound barrier of life and its challenges?

I would ask myself these questions during some of the darker points of my life. Would you believe me if I told you I struggled to find enough motivation to write this chapter based on the gems provided? I stated in the introduction that, as I wrote this book, you have lived and experienced it with me. This book wasn't just conceived in one moment, but through many life moments that were good and not so good. The physical manifestation you are holding and pumping life into your vision's veins is as alive in this book as your body.

There were moments when I had no drive to write another word for this book, let alone complete it. As I sat in my grandparents' den on the eve of Thanksgiving 2017, thinking about finishing this book, the idea of this chapter dawned on me. At that moment, I knew the keys I had pre-written in my notes wouldn't match my current state of mind and mood. I was in a war between borderline depression and mustering up enough fight to finish this race. Remember that I said the race is not a marathon nor a sprint, and whoever tells you that to motivate you has never been driven. The race is a never-ending pursuit of victories with no finish line. In what manner and method you finish the race is equally and at the same time more important than how you prepare when starting the race.

I had daunting battles between focusing on my current situation, which was only temporary tribulations and practicing what I preached in my writings. As I was washing my face and brushing my teeth in preparation to take a physical for a job, I realized that motivation was not the end-all needed to push through the tough times. There are two thoughts I want to highlight in this chapter:

1. The dangers of being motivated and needing the motivation to break barriers.

2. The importance of being driven—as this is what drives success!

How often have you been motivated to go to the next level when you don't even know what is required to get to that level? How do you know what to look for that confirms you're at the next level? I can raise my hand to that … and tell you from experience why you haven't seen it.

When I looked up the definition of motivation, two words grabbed my attention: "the act." From my perspective, motivation is an act that requires willpower and more action than acting. After reading this, many who are motivated daily or seasonally will view the need for motivation differently. The danger of motivation as an act is that it is temporal; there is no endurance at the root for one to attach oneself to. The action part of what is required to be driven stems from motivation not being just an act but an action.

Motivation alone can't adapt to the trying times and barriers that impede vision. Motivation will not suffice when you've reached the lowest form of self-confidence, self-care, self-love, and self-compassion.

KEY V: Be Driven, Not Motivated

Please understand that motivation will not get you off the couch; only reaching for the fire-stick remote will.

I've had countless moments of being motivated, and it was only an act at best almost every time. So, how do you respond after the motivational fix has worn off? For example, consider how many people striving for "vertical living" pay thousands of dollars to attend conferences and seminars headlined by motivational speakers (act). Yet, they never consistently use the principles taught to see results (action) firmly. I would compare it to the passage of scripture that talks about the parable of the Sower:

> **Matthew 13:5 NASB**
> Others fell on the rocky places,
> where they did not have much soil;
> and immediately they sprang up,
> because they had no depth of soil.
> But when the sun had risen, they were scorched;
> and because they had no root, they withered away.

> **Matthew 13:20 NASB (Parable Explained)**
> The one on whom seed was sown on the rocky places,
> this man hears the word and immediately receives it joyfully.
> Yet, he has no firm root in himself but is only temporary,
> and when affliction or persecution arises because
> of the word, he immediately falls away.

This, for me, and I'm hoping for you, is an example of people seeking motivation, such as attending all the conferences and purchasing all the self-help material. Or those who log massive hours on YouTube watching motivating videos or listening to audiobooks and podcasts never apply the material to their personal and professional lives. Don't get me wrong; a select few take what is presented and act upon it to improve. But for the other 99%, they fall away because they have no roots, no clear vision, are not driven when challenges arise, and the high is gone. We've all been there before.

I know I have. There have been plenty of times I was hyped off something new—instead, it has been an idea or new pursuit—or something new presented to me that is supposed to change my life or even became inspired by someone else's testimony that they've turned into motivational content. The problem is that I didn't encounter the challenges they faced or learn how to overcome them. Everyone's experience and how they respond are different, right? How can I live someone else's experience and high-achieving results when I haven't even learned how to conquer my challenges? There was no root established in my journey, so when pressure arises because I've only been motivated, I don't have the endurance or perseverance to see it through. We must be driven!

We can take it further by discussing how short-lived being "motivated" can be for a person. For example, how often have you attended an event designed to motivate and improve you or been in a personal/professional development environment without taking notes or writing down what the speaker suggested?

I'm for sure guilty of that! But, leading up to attending the conference, I was pumped and knew this would be the turning point of my dreams becoming a reality. (Notice: I use the term dreams because I wasn't a visionary when I was motivated).

I can remember having many spurts of catching the motivation high and being disciplined in certain areas of my life—eagerly ready to apply the daily rituals of prominent motivational speakers to my life. The problem I was experiencing during those spurts was that the same thing driving them to motivate me wasn't helping me become driven. Eventually, the motivation would wear off. If motivation were needed to push me through, it would be short-lived. Let me be clear that conferences, self-help material, and personal development from others do

KEY V: Be Driven, Not Motivated

serve a great purpose so long as it's not an act but backed by action. I'm implying that there is a next step that surpasses the motivation that you will need: to become driven. Being driven replaced the need to require motivation to make life happen.

To add, there are a few channels on YouTube that consistently bring it to the motivation department. One to highlight is Eric Thomas. You will need something more than motivation to break the sound barrier of life. More often, motivation only serves as a quick high to get you headed in the right direction and to get you started on the path you desire to accomplish; you'll soon find out that motivation alone doesn't have the longevity to keep you steady in reaching that 768-mph force to breakthrough life's barriers.

When reaching your vision and exceeding it, you need more than videos, conferences, and past failures to give you the juice to make it happen. Some people have the "I need to prove myself" syndrome for motivation, while others need to prove themselves to society, old neighborhoods, and peers to feel like they're tapping into success. But, again, these are still not enough!

Motivation is insufficient to get you through those dry spells, mental setbacks, rejection, and doors closing in your face. Take a quick inventory of when you quit on your marriage, a project, a goal, or an ambitious pursuit in the past. If there's been a time you did quit, I'm sure at this point of the book, one leading cause was because you possibly ran out of motivation.

You can distinguish between those who will be denied and those who refuse to be denied. As I wrote this chapter, I was right there, almost accepting being denied. I was willing to allow defeat to beat me down and keep me defeated; my focus was on looking for more motivation when I should've been drawing on what DRIVES me.

At that time, I was no longer watching Eric Thomas videos on YouTube. I didn't have the energy to listen to more audiobooks on leadership and personal development courses. I wasn't about to pick up another book to motivate me. I had to fall back on my WHY and how that would get me back on the trajectory of obtaining my vision.

Your WHY drives you … and the passion behind your WHY will encourage you to be more driven to bounce back when needed. I learned this critical principle from ET (Eric Thomas) during my season of truly locking in with his material on YouTube.

Webster defines "driven" as *having a compulsive or urgent quality: a driven sense of obligation.* The moment you tap into what drives you, you'll be unstoppable and able to get through every red light of life. To be driven requires more than just essential qualities, but an urgent quality created within you due to one of our more pivotal keys: capitalizing on your life experiences.

Remember that you are no longer content with "C" work but are always compulsive to do better than "A" work.

This is only accomplished by having a driven why for your actions. It took me until my oldest daughter was 12 years old to realize why I should keep a job and hustle my butt off to create space and opportunity to replace my job with a career in music, acting, and entrepreneurship. Realizing that my daughter directly reflected me and my responsibility, I was reminded that she, including her siblings, was my obligation. Becoming more conscious of her well-being became of great importance to me. I knew she depended on my why. I had to boss up!

Looking back to where I am now, I can perceive why I've had so many jobs; when you work for yourself and have no solid reason, it's easy to quit a job to get another, only to repeat the same vicious cycle. You're only working for yourself. This is being self-centered, which only serves you.

If you relate to this, you can see why you quit on many things you started in your life. When only being motivated by self, it's easy to quit on yourself … and even more so, to quit on others. That's because our human nature is set to SELFISH by default.

KEY V: Be Driven, Not Motivated

When you're driven, you think about those counting on you to complete every task you set out to do. Having a "driven why" gives you next-level inspiration; being driven is a compulsive passion that eliminates the need to seek out motivation.

Once you have become driven, you only use motivational tools to improve your skillset; you don't need them to keep you going. People who are motivated *need* inspiration; people who are driven can inspire. Motivated people need an alarm clock to wake them up; results are what wake driven people up every day.

Have you ever been the type of person who only turns it on when it seems beneficial for you?

If so, then you've been a person who has always relied on or needed some form of motivation in doing so. People who tap into being driven always keep it turned on because the benefits far exceed being motivated by self-centered things. I can only speak on this because I'm still learning and developing not to be a selfish person. I'm still fighting the temptations of frequently quitting on others and only being motivated to help or be available to people because of what it would do for me.

Being driven is to thrust yourself to the next level of the God-given vision—that only God has allowed you to envision. Being driven will not only help you become a successful visionary and experience "vertical living" but will also enable you to improve in many vital areas of your life. You'll also focus less on being impressive and more on being impactful.

You'll become dedicated to being more responsible in life decisions; you'll see massive gains of commitment to your family and community; lastly, you'll be a better steward of all that God will and has made you a ruler over.

Suppose you genuinely apply the concepts of this chapter and begin to witness the results in your life. In that case, you'll never plan on quitting on anything again ... not because I said it, but, more importantly, because you'll be too DRIVEN not to believe it and let it happen!

KEY VI: Exceed Expectations of the Opposition

It is my most sincere desire for my readers to reach a place of purposeful and prosperous vision. However, for this to happen, you must be prepared for the antagonistic opposition that will undoubtedly come your way.

During your journey toward your vision, you must not only compete with but *exceed the expectations of your opposition*. Therefore, it's imperative to muster up all your driven passion dwelling inside your core to outhustle, out-endure, and out-perform the opposition.

The opposition is not just those individuals you compete against daily for the coveted prize of winning. Still, you're also competing against self-doubt, idleness, procrastination, and the CCs (complacency and comfortability). These are some of your most fabulous and fierce forms of competition, and you must *exceed their expectations*! They will battle, fight, distract, disrupt, and war with you when you decide to be great and reach your vision until you expire.

Here are three main reasons you must exceed the expectations of the opposition:

1. The opposition is relentless and never tires in its pursuit to impede and hinder your path toward your vision.
2. The opposition expects you to underperform, start, stop, and grow weary in your well-doing.
3. The opposition has high expectations of you failing due to fear, self-doubt, idleness, procrastination, being distracted, lacking willpower, depletion of self-discipline, little to no faith, and being comfortable with mediocrity.

We are our most fierce competition in every form of competition. Bringing back to your attention the children of Israel from the bible, it's easy to recognize how their easy four-day journey turned into a despairing 40-year pilgrimage. It wasn't just disobedience and a lack of faith in God that extended their journey; the leading factor was that *they couldn't exceed becoming their opposition.* The children of Israel couldn't cross over into the Promised Land because they were in their way. Fear, a lack of faith, and self-doubt became a giant standing in their way. Greed, selfishness, and impatience often give the opposition a considerable advantage, even if reciprocated.

This same concept happens to you, being your biggest competition; only you can stop yourself. Only what you grant power can dominate and defeat you. If you lose control, it's because you first lost control, not anybody else. You mistakenly let an external factor cause and create an internal reaction that gave the opposition a decisive edge.

This comes into play in all forms of life and competition. Suppose you allow rough conditions, trials, and trying moments to get the upper hand in your flight to vertical living. In that case, you'll only reach your promised destination if you exceed your expectations. Preparing and preventative measures are the most underrated and least-used techniques

KEY VI: Exceed Expectations of the Opposition

when executing. If you poorly prepare for a fight, you'll perform poorly when it's time to compete ... not even coming close to winning.

If you lose a 100-meter race due to unfocused training, it won't be that you lost to the winner first; you first failed yourself by not correctly training. The person who finished first was prepared to place first; the person who came in second was, unfortunately, the first loser of the race. In professional competition, anything after first place is not a win. Also, I believe the experience is not the same in life. You won't always finish in first place, but if you stay in the arena competing, you'll always allow yourself to seize victory for YOU! Success is truly whatever you deem it to be.

One example I'd like to use of how a person can be in their way is like the friend of an individual caught stealing, along with a couple of their associates. (I call them associates because real friends aren't encouraging others to steal). Your associates wouldn't be at fault that you got caught stealing; it will ultimately be your fault that you're in trouble with the law. The person who got caught stealing was in their way. The power of choice and decision meets everything in life along with its effects, and we must always answer to whatever the consequences of that powerful choice bring us.

The point I'm making is that anything you allow to place you in a non-beneficial predicament starts with you being in the way of yourself.

> *You are your most significant competitor.*
> *You dictate whether a win or loss comes your way.*
> *You either need to meet your expectations or*
> *exceed the expectations of your opposition.*

So, how do you succeed in exceeding the expectations of the opposition? I don't honestly think that you can. But you must recognize the need to exceed your negative expectations and realize how easily hostile they become.

I intensely experienced these barriers and struggles during my life while writing this book. Believing the negative expectations I put on myself and living up to them urged me to do everything opposite the successful, positive principles I was learning. During this crossroad, I could feel the ferocious hammering of everything negative from every angle, never letting up off the gas. Finally, however, some very dark, depressing, and tragic moments forced me to outhustle, out-endure, and out-perform the opposition of myself. *The battle truly starts in the mind.*

Believe me when I tell you there was an epic clash within myself that required everything to apply what I shared with you to finish this book. I can't take any credit for what it took and what led to the success and completion of this book. All the praise, glory, and honor go to God and His amazing grace to allow me to grow through it so I can get to it … not just for the book, but life itself.

The opposition of your*self* will be challenging and tiring, but there is another test you'll face on top of this one. That test is the one of tolerating, with love and patience, the opposition from negative people.

If allowed to do so, people and their words can dismantle and shipwreck your ability to stay on your vision course. You must out-endure your opposition and consistently stay driven in your life pursuits. You must tire out the opposition by being positively long-winded. Never allow the opposition of negative people, their bitterness, and cruel intentions to break you down. Never let a person's discouraging or critical words stop you when you've been armed with these keys to vertical living.

The vision God gave you is more powerful than any opinion one single individual can have about you. Eve could not complete the mission and vision God had already set for her life because she exchanged the truth for a lie. Eve exchanged the truth God had already told her for the lie Satan had promised her. There's a stark difference between what you already have been given and what you've been told you'll receive.

KEY VI: Exceed Expectations of the Opposition

Satan already had an opinion about Eve; she was fragile and could be easily manipulated. He also established a particular idea about Adam—that he was weak and would not put up a fight.

During your journey toward your vision, remember the truth about your abilities; don't allow the opinion of another to cause you to deviate from your life-purposed trip. Reflecting on some principles from Key I about *making fear your tailwind* is a perfect response to criticism. It doesn't matter if it's negative, critical, or constructive. When drawing back on that key, you can take any of the three and make them work for you and not against you.

Adam and Eve were created in God's expressed image and likeness (Genesis 1:27 NASB). However, Satan took the truth and made it a half-truth lie by restating what God had already said and done—but instead by twisting the truth for his agenda.

In this life, you must live by and stick to the truth about yourself, what you believe, and what you stand on. For example, if you know you're great, don't allow someone to convince you that you're only good. Instead, stick to those ideas and beliefs that make you great, not the opinion of another that makes you seem less than.

My last principle on how you can and will exceed the expectations of the opposition is what I learned from my good friend, YouTube hero Cedric Thompson Jr. During his collegiate football career, he would wear an armband that read AO1. I found it advantageous for myself and believe sharing with you would become beneficial. I challenge you to incorporate the AO1 mentality to outperform the opposition consistently.

I would dub this the AO1 factor. I'm sure at this point you're yelling, "Spill it already! What does AO1 mean?"

Cedric and I share the same faith regarding Jesus Christ, so all that we do it for is for an Audience of One (AO1)—Jesus Christ and family. You can choose how and what you want this to mean or reflect your

AO1. And, again, that may not be your belief system and certainly isn't a pre-requisite for this principle and idea to be applied in your life to exceed the expectations of the opposition.

Whether you consider that "audience" to be your peers, your kids, or your wife, the biggest reason a person must have an AO1 mentality is that no matter how great or how difficult the task set before you is when you are performing for an audience of one, you're able to block out thoughts of underperforming or failure. This happens because you're not concerned with the opinions and expectations of the crowd, social media, or people in general. At that moment, your only other concern is showing up to perform at a high level.

When I agree to a booking for a performance or headlining a show, I never ask what the size of the crowd will be. If I were concerned with numbers, I would probably never do any shows; instead, I would allow attendance to dictate what I'm passionate about doing anyway. However, with the AO1 factor, I'm hitting the stage for much bigger reasons, and I will give 120%, whether it's five or 50,000 people. I'm going to give it my all because, in my mind, there's only one audience: Christ and my family. I know that Christ and my family are there with and for me.

I want you to remember this because it will encourage you to give your best as often as possible. Unlike everybody else, those who support you want to see you win in life and don't care about results.

You, too, must find your inner AO1 in all your life pursuits to properly focus on the task and consistently drown out all the unnecessary noise, distractions, and negativity that will attempt to derail you from the vision. When you have found your *AO1* and who in all that you do, then the negative expectations of the opposition will never discourage you from obtaining "vertical living." Ever again!

KEY VII:
No Thought is Insignificant

> "Become what you will be, not what you are."

Wow, what a journey it has been, my friend! I don't know about you, but I feel as though we've bonded through these seven keys to vertical living.

I intentionally saved this key as my last because I thought highly of you; your development was more important than writing this book for my gain. I truly did this for you. Notice the title and power of this key and what you just read:

"I thought highly of you"! This brings me to the seventh key:

> *No Thought is Insignificant.*

Proverb 23:7 NASB says, "As a man thinks in his heart, so is he." At this point in your life, much of what has occurred—good or not so good—has been a product of what you've been thinking and your thoughts about yourself. What you are now is not what you'll become later; who you are now is only what you've thought about yourself until now.

Let me share another life thought with you. Proverbs 18:21NASB says, "Life and death are in the power of the tongue." What you say about yourself and how you feel about yourself will control, dictate, and set forth who you are, what you'll become, and the life you'll live.

"Thoughts are causes; conditions are effects! You become what you think."

Pay attention! Not only does what you say and think to establish who you will become, but it also controls the behavior of your environment, the condition of your livelihood, and even your state of health (mentally & physically). Just as we have discovered how powerful fear is, it is the same with thoughts and words. Your thoughts can initiate sickness or healing, poverty or prosperity, mental stability, or mental breakdown.

Insignificant thoughts often are so small and come into being so quickly that you don't even realize that you've had thousands of thoughts in seconds—some positive and a majority negative. Regardless of where they are on the scale of positivity and negativity, *none of those thoughts were insignificant*. I recommend setting a goal and routine to practice, minimize, and diminish negative thinking. When referring to yourself and what you desire to achieve, never loosely or unconsciously say words or begin a sentence such as "I got this **little** idea," "I'm going **to try**," "I **would** start doing XYZ," "I **might**," etc. Every bolded word used negatively impacts your pursuit of vertical living.

Think of every conversation you've had saying things like this. As innocently and naturally as they sound, those words were harmful bombs destroying your vision. If you knew your business would only scale to narrow results, you would never let such a thought become words. Give maximum purposeful intention to this mentality and way of thinking; it must be a practiced application. So those bolded words must be changed to AMAZING, I WILL, I MUST, and I AM.

So, just how powerful are our thoughts?

For example, imagine you just walked into a major corporation for a life and career-changing interview. While waiting in a decked-out

KEY VII: No Thought is Insignificant

lobby surrounded by three other candidates, you notice one of the interviewees is wearing an expensive tailor-made suit. So, naturally, your initial thoughts begin to race.

Some of those thoughts sound like this:

- "He's going to get the job."
- "I don't look professional enough."
- "I bet his resume is off the charts."
- "He'll probably get called first."
- "My suit is nothing compared to his."

None of those thoughts are insignificant. Even if the one thinking of them ignores them, they carry way more power than you might imagine. What has begun to happen is that those thoughts are creating a reality for you and your environment. These thoughts will serve as an advantage for the interviewee in the tailor-made suit and a disadvantage for you.

Seeing that you have thought more highly of the other candidate than yourself, you'll more likely botch the interview and make room for getting the job easier for the candidate you were praising in your thoughts. Because of your thinking, you're creating a disadvantage for yourself and painting a picture of future expectations that will later cause you to sink into even more despair and anxiety. This thinking will affect how you perform during the interview.

And it all started with your thoughts.

Allow positive thoughts to transform you, disarming negative thoughts to conform to you. For example, the book of Genesis details God creating the heavens and earth. At the end of each day of creation, God always concluded and confirmed by saying, *"It was good."*

Michael Jordan always considered himself a champion before winning his first championship. Getting there was a very long and challenging road, but he never changed his thoughts about becoming a champion. MJ became what he thought. You must physically buy into what you're mentally selling for the vision to become a reality.

Before the chair you're sitting in became a physical chair, it was a thought in someone's mind. Before becoming an author, I had to think about what to write and envision the book's completion in my mind first. I had to buy into the idea that I'm an author without having written a single page of the book. You know my motto: SEE IT. BELIEVE IT. BECOME IT.

You must ponder what to become first before you can be. I never knew I was an author until someone put the thought in my mind. I would be asked questions during moments of sharing my testimony at events: The very next response at some point would be, "When are you going to write that book"? Other times, I would be told, "You should write a book," because of the blogs I post on WordPress.

The thoughts those people had about me and the words they shared with me were so powerful that they assisted me in creating the very book you're holding. I'm sure they thought nothing of it when sharing those thoughts with me but remember: *no thought is insignificant, even in receiving those thoughts.*

So, do me a solid, and please stop brushing off significant thoughts and what you think about yourself as insignificant. If you think negative, you'll reap negative; if you think positive, you'll reap positive. If you want to change your world, then change your words. This all starts with how you feel first and think overall.

Insignificant thoughts pose an even more significant threat when charged negatively. Along with negative thoughts come fear, self-doubt, diminished confidence, etc. When negative thoughts are treated as significant consistently, they can welcome many ailments like depression, stress, and anxiety. All these can lead to increased chances of health issues, a quitter's mentality, and soured relationships. This all starts with you and your thoughts.

KEY VII: No Thought is Insignificant

Your thoughts confirm how you feel about yourself and others. If the wrong ideas are conceived, you can cause harm to yourself and others. For example, if you think alcohol will solve your internal problems, you'll likely become an alcoholic; if you think saving money will lead to a life-changing vacation, you'll save like never before and take that dream vacation. The way we think will either build us up or break us down.

> *"Only feed on and be fueled off the positive thoughts of people's opinions about you."* —Iso

You must be exceedingly sharp in your disciplines and preparedness for anything because if you're not ready, you can quickly aid in destroying yourself, or others will destroy you. It's bad enough how easy it is to think negatively about yourself, but how much more difficult it would be to recover if you considered the negative thoughts of what others say and think about you.

It is said that within the science and mental health community, people have an average of 12,000–60,000 thoughts daily. Of those, about 98% of those thoughts carry over from the previous day, while 80% of all those thoughts are negative. Based on those numbers, it's a sure bet that if you had a bad day on Monday, those negative thoughts would await you before bed and wake up with you on Tuesday morning.

In key I, I talked about how exigent it is to have a renewed mind to see your vision and become your vision, enabling you to experience it and obtain the joy that comes from living vertically. This same technique of a renewed mind must also be applied to changing how you think and what thoughts you allow to occupy space in your mind.

No thought that became a reality and benefited you is ever insignificant in any outcome. If you allow ideas not conducive to your vision and transformation to roam free, you'll become precisely what you don't want to experience. So often, people allow evil thoughts to roam free for so long that they become captive and enslaved to a reality of negative thoughts.

This is where a person can truly reflect the experiences and struggles of what they're going through. Trying times are likely the greatest obstacle a person faces when consistently producing significant thoughts. Yet so many individuals allow what they see in front of them to forecast how they'll think, feel, and react in the *current present, thus affecting their coming future.*

Don't get me wrong; I completely understand how difficult it is to produce positive thoughts when times are at their worst. I know how easy it is to submit and bow down to negative thinking. My remedy for that would be to *take those thoughts captive, dwell on the good things in your life, and, more importantly, overwhelm yourself with optimism.*

We often take these things for granted daily: good health, food to eat, shelter, a warm shower, and our devoted and loving spouse—all things we consider bare minimum or just routine and insignificant are, in fact, vitally important to our life. Imagine if any of those qualities of life were removed from your life. How different not just your thoughts would be, but how different your very life would be.

> *"Exchange insignificant thoughts for significant thinking."* —Iso

This is an essentially practical approach; you could practice conquering negative thoughts. When you've reached a rough patch in life, think back on a similar situation and the eventual good that came about or how you pushed through it.

Once you've remembered the good, draw on some of the techniques and processes you applied that got you through it. Another practice would be to do something you fully enjoy. What can you participate in that separates you from the problem, burden, or stress? When you think differently, you'll act differently!

KEY VII: No Thought is Insignificant

> *Focus on the solution, not the situation*

Find positive environments you can interact with that will help reshape your thinking. For example, one crucial practice I learned from my mentor, friend, and business partner Evan Howard was doing an act of kindness. He found joy and relief during one of the most challenging moments of his life by gifting me his MacBook Pro.

Evan thought about how much I would benefit from it, but more importantly, he thought about how much joy it would bring me … and, in return, the joy he would receive within himself by acting on it. (Think differently; ACT differently.) The thought of giving me the MacBook, which could've been registered as insignificant, served an even greater purpose as it was the start of how I could type the manuscript for the very book you're holding.

We've been conditioned that only money and success shape our world and will bring about happiness in difficult times. Yet, it is our inner thoughts that create the money and success in the world we live in. I know that for me to succeed, I must think about success. To maintain joy, I must think vertically and create joy for myself and others. To get through trials and tribulations victoriously, I must routinely dwell on the small wins and victories I've experienced.

In addition, I must exchange lies for truth rather than vice versa. When I feel the burdens of life and my outward perception attempts to convince me that this is my reality, I take that lie and exchange it for truth, such as reading one of my favorite go-to Bible passages:

"'For I know the plans and thoughts that I have for you,' says the Lord, 'plans for peace and well-being and not for disaster, to give you a future and a hope.'" (Jerimiah 29:11 AMP)

If God has beautiful thoughts and plans for you to prosper and succeed, why should you let what you're going through create something contrary?

> *Think differently, and you'll live differently; no thought is ever insignificant!*

Final Thoughts

> *"You can have more than you got because you can become more than what you are."*
> —Jim Rohm

If I can write and publish a book, and you read the book, then we both can execute, complete, and repeat anything we want to do in life.

As I was able to construct this book and arrive at my final thoughts, I instantly had a feeling of genuine satisfaction and gratefulness. My heart began to race because I knew that in reaching this point of the book, I made it without quitting.

This type of reading content should be no less than a couple hundred pages, but it was about quality over quantity. I'd still be an author if I only wrote and published ten pages. But, on the other hand, what good is it to have over 300 pages of empty words?

I hope this book reminded you of how great you are. I didn't need to persuade or convince you of what was already known; I just had to remind you of what you may have forgotten or bring to your attention what you didn't realize.

The takeaway is that you've never lost anything; I just had to help you find what you've been looking for. The most significant advantage you now have over others is that I've helped awaken the sleeping and successful giant in you.

No longer are you dreaming your life away, but you're now alive to your vision.

Your vision is evident at this point. The difference between my book and all the other books is that I'm not selling you anything. I'm not convincing you to follow specific methods and techniques to duplicate unrealistic results such as riches, fame, and insane success. I'm not sold on success anymore but more on attaining vertical living. My mission has been completed by presenting you with a gift in this book and introducing another side of perspective and application for you to benefit from. *You're Not High Enough* was not a book designed to give you any cheat codes or shortcuts to success, but instead to provide you with keys to living vertically regardless of what you do for the rest of your life.

You will benefit from this read because your life will never be the same, and I, in return, will help because I was able to reach, affect, and impact just one person. Every page you read now allows you to write a page for yourself, your children, your community, and your world.

I feel so privileged and honored that God has allowed me this opportunity. I feel so grateful that you allowed me to share this moment with you.

You now have a powerful tool at your disposal to create your vision and share that vision with others. You, my friend, have become a book you can display and create a positive, purposeful, and productive image for others.

You have a story to tell, not millions, but just one person needs to know, see, and hear it.

I challenge you to never settle on a dream but to strive and invest in your vision.

These seven major keys presented in this book will impact, enhance, and improve your life personally, professionally, mentally, financially,

Final Thoughts

and spiritually. There is no doubt in my mind that I'll be reading your book soon.

With God, all things are POSSIBLE AND FACTUAL!

Thank you, and God bless!

Words I Live By

"Effective people are on time; IMPACTFUL people are early." —ISO

"Add to your fortune when you become more VALUABLE." —ISO

"Get the results of LIFE or lose lives failing! —ISO

"Be results-driven!" —ISO

"Make life happen for you; don't let it happen to you." —ISO

"There's more to the ledge than just jumping off" —ISO

"Why are known Hopeless Landfills preferable to strange heavens?" —Les Brown

"Learn, make mistakes; learn from made mistakes, keep learning!" —Tim Grover

"Godly wisdom trumps might (strength); labor (hard productive work)." —Author unknown

"Diligence, organization, time utilization, and resourcefulness produce way better results than strength alone." —Author unknown

"All life forms strive to reach their maximum potential, except human beings, because of choice. Look at the trees; they never half-grow. We choose to survive or thrive!" —Author unknown

"There's a right type of instinct and a wrong type of impulse: Be instinctive, not impulsive!" —Author unknown

Dedication Page

I want to dedicate this personal and life-changing achieve-ment to my Lord & Savior, Jesus Christ, without whom this would not have been possible.

To all my kiddos. My super Sonic nephew Ivan. You all are my biggest WHY for what I do and have been able to accomplish. I also want to thank the two mothers of my kids, Jasmine & Victoria, for excellently picking up my slack in raising our kids.

My favorite sister in the world, India! I still believe she's older than me by how she took care of me. You've always considered me in every phase of our lives and have been a super dope sister. I love you, "Stinky Pot"! To my wonderful grandparents, Gerorg'o and Grams, who have never let me down, EVER! Dad and Mom, I wouldn't be the person I am today without you two. You both have been the backbone of who I've become. All the sacrifices were made to ensure my life was the best possible. Thank you both for shaping and molding me to be greater than statistics suggest.

Evan Howard—my mentor, business partner, and more brother than a friend –always believed in every vision and thought I cooked up. Thank you for never giving up on me and constantly pushing me to improve. I want to thank Mr. Carter, my coach; if it weren't for him, I wouldn't be able to proudly call myself an alum of Sinclair Community College.

Tony Rogers, bro, you have inspired me and given me even more confidence to complete this book. During our back-and-forth of audio text messages, I wouldn't have been able to define what vertical living means. Thank you, bro!

To my family, all my cousins, friends, ex-gang members, hustlers, barbers, Lavish Boi Gang crew, Corey & Marsune, Colonel White H.S., and the city of Dayton, Ohio, thank you for many challenging life experiences that helped me build toughness and an edge I wouldn't have received anywhere else in the world.

To every employer who took a chance to hire me, allowing me to benefit from the skills and knowledge gained. Thank you for allowing me to recognize that I was never born to be a 9-5 employee but was only designed and called to CREATE.

I want to thank Overcomers in Christ Ministries, the church, and my family of believers who helped me establish a genuinely intimate relationship with the Lord.

Thank you, Mama'O, for trusting your gut and taking a chance on me when I first moved to Los Angeles and allowing me to set up shop in your newly renovated living room when I had nowhere else to go. I am grateful to you, Lon6z, for helping me improve and instilling the know-how to see plans through. Thank you to my editor, Bonita Jewel, for providing me with your editing and polishing skills. Thank you, Lorie DeWorken, for adding the finishing touches to include a fantastic book presentation. Lastly, I want to thank the city of Los Angeles for such an experience that gave me the much-added fuel to start & finish this book. Love you all!

How to stay in contact and for booking speaking engagements:

Email: inspire@splashsocietyinc.com
Instagram: @th3kidwavie

AUTHOR BIO

Lee, also known as "IsoWavie," is an American Recording Music Artist, songwriter, music engineer, and brand content creator from Dayton, OH. Having relocated to Los Angeles, CA, Wavie has released several successful music projects on all streaming platforms, has collaborated with major companies such as Meta, Shutterstock, and TYLNT Inc., and made his acting debut in Hollywood as a background actor appearing in major studio television shows such as All-American: Homecoming, The Goldbergs, HBO's Rap Sh!t, major motion film produced by Snoop Dogg "The Underdogs." Wavie is now penning his experiences, challenges, and growth with his first book release. In the book, Wavie details, with powerful examples, insightful thoughts, and innovative philosophy, vividly how chasing dreams only can lead to nightmarish realities. Wavie says, "My overall goal for the book is for the individual to become elite, wake up to your destined purpose, lead from a servant position, live life vertically, and become increasingly better." Wavie displays great intensity in the book and is passionate to share that once he started having VISION for his life, everything began to go VERTICAL. When I'm not in the studio, creating content, or on set filming, I'm in the gym getting to the gains or in the kitchen preparing my favorite go-to Alaskan salmon and angel hair pasta meal.

www.ingramcontent.com/pod-product-compliance
Lightning Source LLC
Chambersburg PA
CBHW061446040426
42450CB00007B/1242